PROPERTY MILLIONAIRE SECRETS

WITH FREE ticket OFFER!

John LEE | Vincent WONG | Nicola GOHIL

AUTHORS OF THE BEST SELLING
"STEP BY STEP GUIDE TO LEASE OPTIONS"

PUBLISHED BY
WEALTH DRAGONS

Property Millionaire Secrets

Published by:

Wealth Dragons Ltd
Milton Keynes Business Centre
Foxhunter Drive
Linford Wood
Milton Keynes
Buckinghamshire
MK14 6GD

Contact information for request for permission to reproduce or distribute materials available through this book is listed below:

Email: info@wealthdragons.co.uk
Website: www.WealthDragons.co.uk

ISBN: 978-0-9563895-4-1

About The Authors

John Lee is an international speaker and mentor recognised for his vibrant, get-up-and-go style that inject life and emotion in to his events and seminars.

He is co-founder of Wealth Dragons, a company dedicated to helping property investors achieve their financial dreams, and joint author of the first lease options book released in the UK - *"Step-by-Step Guide to Lease Options – No Mortgage, No Deposit No Problem"*.

Today, John trains thousands of students around the world how to create wealth from property investment.

At 21-years-old, John had two ambitions - to earn enough money to not have to work for another boss, and to own a Lamborghini sports car. He achieved both by the age of 27.

Selling and negotiating are second nature to John, giving him the ability to deal with people of all backgrounds. Now, he likes to inspire others by showing them how they can unlock their own potential and take control their financial destiny.

Life was not always so easy for John. As a youngster, he often spent 10 hours a day washing in a restaurant run by his parents, but the dirty dishes, grease and suds did not dilute his passion to work in the film industry.

After university, John became a leading animator, working for five years on top box-office hits like Harry Potter, Despereaux, X-Men and The Transformers.

After putting in long hours and helping make the film producers rich, he quit to set up in business for himself, vowing the money he made would go in to his pocket, not someone else's. Although switching careers, John has not lost his love for TV

About The Authors

and film, and often pops up on TV in shows like Little Britain, Waterloo Road, Byker Grove, and Coronation Street.

When he first left the world of film, John sold everything, including his car, to raise cash to fund his education in property investment.

This education laid a solid foundation that let him build a successful property business. John is a keen believer in improving self-development through education and experience. Like a sponge, he soaks up new information and techniques all the time – but his ability is not just acquiring facts, but showing others how to apply that knowledge to their financial advantage.

John has a unique speaking style that resonates within people at the deepest level to spur then in to action. His aim is to show them how to create personal wealth.

John's outlook on life is not to have wishes but goals.

Vincent Wong is a master of generating sales leads. In the past two years, more than 45,000 motivated sellers wanting to sell their homes have responded to his marketing messages.

Those leads have bought property worth more than £10.8 million for Vincent and his fellow investors. At the core of his work ethic is a blend of professionalism and integrity.

Vincent was a speaker at T Harv Eker's Never Work Again personal excellence event in Singapore and continues to help students around the world learn his techniques in lead generation and closing property deals. An MBA, Vincent co-founded Wealth Dragons and was joint author of *"Step-by-Step guide to Lease Options – No Mortgage, No Deposit, No Problem"*.

About The Authors

Vincent gave up a six-figure salary and comfortable career as a pharmacist to start out on his own. His motivation was to spend more time with his family – especially his daughter, the then three-year-old Hannah.

Long working hours led to Vincent spending time away from home, and he felt a change was needed for all their sakes. Life is never that easy, and Vincent travelled down several dead-ends before finding success – hence his motto is never give up.

A successful mentor and businessman, Vincent remains humble and dedicates time to guiding others to financial freedom.

Many of his case studies are based on personal experience. Vincent encourages investors to take action and believes success is not only measured by wealth, but by how you help others achieve their goals.

Vincent is married to Annika, and has two children - Hannah and Lewis.

 **Nicola Gohil** is the "brain-child" behind the systems of Wealth Dragons. Before she became financially free in 2005, Nicola's nine-to-five job involved working on multi-million pound projects in London as a senior project manager for blue-chip clients such as Diageo, Triumph, Virgin Trains, British Airways, Nike, Ladbrokes and Sony.

Alongside her job, Nicola would work, all hours flat out investing in property. In 2005 she gave up her job to become a full time property developer and investor.

As a young woman, she initially struggled to overcome prejudices in the building industry. In the end, she had no choice but to learn trades such as plumbing, bricklaying and tiling herself.

About The Authors

Working on property developments gave Nicola an insight in to putting together winning teams of builders that contributed to her business success.

Her passion, determination and tenacity helped her win and complete several multi-million pound property projects that gave Nicola financial freedom.

Within two years of leaving her job, she became a multi-millionaire.

Now, she acts as a consultant for Wealth Dragons, drawing from her experience to advise on diverse topics like property auctions, landlord knowledge, splitting leases, commercial property, extending homes and flat conversions.

Nicola also supports speaking tours for the Wealth Dragons in the UK, Singapore, Hong Kong, Europe, Malaysia, Australia and New Zealand.

In her spare time, Nicola supports charity work for orphanages in India.

YOUR FREE TICKET

valid from the 1st March 2011 - 1st March 2012

Wealth Dragons Unleashed

- How to find motivated sellers
- How to negotiate 25% discounts
- How to use Lease Options
- How to create multiple income streams in property

Prepaid Entry Ticket
Terms & Conditions Apply

Go to this website to secure your free ticket: http://www.WealthDragons.co.uk/ticketoffer.html

— WEALTH DRAGONS —
UNLEASHED
THE POWER OF KNOWLEDGE & NETWORKING

A Hot Date With The Wealth Dragons

Breathe fire in to your property business by spending some time with the Wealth Dragons.

Wealth Dragon Unleashed events are a series of themed meetings designed to enhance your property skills by providing the knowledge and tools you need to boost your profits.

Joining Wealth Dragons Unleashed puts you on a short-cut to success while letting you learn from the experiences of property professionals and other like-minded investors in a friendly, risk-free environment.

Wealth Dragons Unleashed is the place to network and share knowledge and contacts for any serious property investor - whether they are setting out or already manage an extensive portfolio.

Wealth Dragons Unleashed events run all over the UK and competition for places is fierce – so be sure to book your place early.

Visit www.WealthDragons.co.uk/Event.html
to book your place at Wealth Dragons Unleashed

Contents

Chapter 1

The Two Types Of Investors

◇◇

In this chapter:

- *Deal or no deal – buying from estate agents*
- *Paying the full price is never right*
- *Revealing Property Millionaire Secret #1*

◇◇

Property investors come in many shapes and sizes, but only two mind sets – professionals who act a certain way and have a recession-proof business and the rest, who speculate and tend to make money only in a rising market.

Many of these newbies and amateurs made money before the credit crunch because property generally forgives mistakes during buoyant times.

When the going is tougher, like our experience in more recent years, investors cannot rely on their luck or a rising market to bail them out of trouble.

Intelligent investors need strategies that make money regardless of how the market performs.

A starting point for building a robust property business is finding out how not to buy property.

Deal or no deal – buying from estate agents

Mention buying a home and the first place most newbie investors consider looking is an estate agent or an online property portal, like Rightmove.

The power of marketing leads them to believe estate agents and their online equivalents are the only way to source decent property deals.

A Wealth Dragon knows better. A Wealth Dragon is not mesmerised by a few colourful images and description that says more about the number of plug points in a room than the letting and profit potential.

Inexperienced property investors will take the bait.

They will make an offer and haggle as if they were buying a cheap souvenir from a holiday bazaar.

If the property is listed at £100,000, they try an offer of £95,000 or £90,000, and think they have negotiated a deal on acceptance.

What these investors do not realise is that the £100,000 is an asking price that the estate agent has recommended to the seller.

Listen carefully and you will hear the estate agent say 'a price we can achieve'. The property is not worth that price, the value is just a figure the estate agent feels someone will pay.

Under those circumstances, negotiating a discount from the asking price is hardly a deal at all.

Paying the asking price is never right

The next step is financing the deal.

Chapter 1 - The Two Types of Investor

The usual route is approaching a bank or building society personally or making an application through a mortgage broker. Either way, the mortgage amount is generally a percentage of the property valuation. In the trade this is called the LTV or loan-to-value.

For a while, in the heady heights of the property boom, some lenders would offer home mortgages for 100% LTV to first-time buyer, especially young professionals or graduates.

At one stage, Northern Rock, the building society turned bank, would lend up to 125% LTV.

Northern Rock was one of the institutions to suffer first and hardest in the credit crunch. Many regard the run on the stricken bank by distraught savers in a panic to withdraw their savings as the blue touch paper that exploded in to recession.

Loan-to-values are inching their way back to the heady heights of 80-85%, but the best interest rates are kept for borrowers with the largest deposits.

If a home is worth £100,000, buy-to-let investors should expect to borrow 75% LTV or £75,000. This leaves an investor to find £25,000 to complete the deal. So, unless a buyer has 25% of the value to put down, the deal is not viable.

OK. So the offer's in and accepted. Our buyer has a mortgage offer, pays the deposit and becomes the proud owner of an investment property.

The trouble is the celebration feels a little flat because the figures do not work out. The buying price does not reflect a deep discount. In fact, the estate agent suggested the owner should bump up the asking price by a few grand to encourage a lower offer that was still acceptable.

Chapter 1 - The Two Types of Investor

Once the keys have exchanged hands, most buyers realise they paid top dollar for their property and wiped out their savings as well. If the property is valued at £100,000, £25,000 is quite a lot of money to find as a deposit.

Mr and Mrs Average, who earn £47,000 a year between them before tax, according to the Office of National Statistics, have to save for a good while to put aside that sort of money. Meanwhile, they probably went without a good few of life's luxuries.

Patience is a virtue for these investors because their profit is in a pot of gold at the end of the house price rainbow.
Their cash is tied up in the property and is released by remortgaging or selling.

The mistake is buying at full price. This locks investors in to a waiting game. Agreed, sooner or later, the market will rise to let the buyer turn a profit, but that is more luck than judgement.

Even then, the profit is taxable. Investors must pay capital gains tax (CGT) on disposal of a property. Taking cash out of the property over and above the initial purchase price by refinancing is just taking an advance on the eventual disposal proceeds.

This is how many novices invest in property – negotiating through an estate agent, paying full price while waiting for the price to increase - and do not forgot the inevitable tax bill.
This is how professional investors do not buy property.

Revealing Property Millionaire Secret #1

If you learn nothing else in property, make this your mantra:

Chapter 1 - The Two Types of Investor

Property Millionaire Secret # 1: Professional investors always make their money when they buy, not by waiting for property price inflation.

In other words, professional property people never pay full price for a property.

If the asking price is £100,000, they will look to seal the deal for £80,000, giving instant equity of £20,000. Equity is the net value of a property after deducting financial charges, like the mortgage.

It is not the same as cash in the bank, but equity is £20,000 that goes in to the credit column to increase an investor's net worth.

What's more releasing some of that equity gives property investors tax-free cash – sometimes with the bonus of setting the charges and interest off against rent received to reduce income tax bills as well.

This is how professional investors complete deals and have the money to go on to buy more property when novices are still stuck at the starting line.

Professional investors buy property at below market value or BMV to unlock the instant equity.

Then, they find a way to release this instant equity by refinancing.

In other words, they have a fast pay-back period for the money they put down without locking their cash in to a deal for the long term.

This lets professional investors to buy a lot of property in a short time. A Wealth Dragon is a professional property investor who looks for instant equity and figures out how to release that cash to fund even more deals.

Wealth Dragons do not rely on estate agents for their leads but make their deals directly with sellers.

Declaration

Stand up and take a deep breath. Put your hand on your heart or point your index fingers to your temples and read out loud:

- **I will not rely on estate agents to find deals**

- **I make money when I buy by creating instant value, not when I sell**

Clench your fist and punch triumphantly in the air and say: "I'm a Wealth Dragon"!

Chapter 2

Avoiding Costly Property Mistakes

In the last chapter, we looked at the number one Property Millionaire Secret.

The next step is the finding out how to avoid the three traps that cost novice investors thousands of pounds.

These are grave mistakes committed by amateurs who have lost money so if you can avoid them, you're half way to succeed! Our lawyer who's had 40 years experience in the market told me he's seen more investors being made bankrupt in the present property cycle due to unscrupulous dealings than any other times.

Mistake 1 – Dealing with unmotivated sellers

Wealth Dragons only deal with motivated sellers.

Time is money, and Wealth Dragons do not have the time to spend with home owners who are not ready to sign on the dotted line.

Who is a motivated seller? The answer is someone who is in a rush to sell because they are under pressure from outside, like a homeowner who is jobless; in debt or who has mortgage arrears and is facing repossession.

At the top of that mental checklist when talking to a seller are a few direct questions to establish their motivation.

The key question is: "Why are you moving?"

A reply should explain why they need to sell quickly and to a Wealth Dragon, this indicates the seller is flexible over the terms and the price.

Mistake 2 – Losing your cool over hotspots

Wealth Dragons play cool over property hot spots. These are places where speculators move in on the back of rumours that an area is about to improve, hoping to buy cheaply and make a quick buck.

Hot spots are fuelled by regeneration plans, new motorways and shopping or leisure developments.

Corby, Northamptonshire, a former was a favourite hot spot on the back of plans to build a rail link to London. Corby had two real claims to fame – one as a steel town until the works closed in 1981 and the other as the largest British town not to have a railway station.

The station linking the town to London St Pancra's opened in February 2009.

The problem comes when a hot spot goes off the boil. Developments are often cancelled for planning or financial reasons – take the recent recession and the decimation of the house building industry. Hot spots are speculative investments.

Many investors did make money in Corby and elsewhere during the property bull market – a time when prices are going up at a fast pace. In a flat or falling market, this speculation is best reserved for novice investors.

Mistake 3 – Flipping was a big flop

Like pinning your hopes on a hot spot, off plan investment is betting on a future outcome that may not materialise.
Off plan investment proved an expensive mistake for most property people.

Investing off plan is buying a property that is not built. Often investors buy from a drawing, hence the term 'off plan' and most of these deals are struck before the footings go down.

The idea is buying cheaply from a developer at the start of phase one of building. As each stage or phase of development progresses, prices generally go up.

Most developments have four phases and the price rises with the start of each phase.

The hope is that investing early means a home will quickly appreciate in value for sale at a profit just before or after the development completes.

Many investors 'flipped' off plan property. Flipping involved putting deposits on one or more homes at an early stage of development and then selling at a higher price in a later phase.

If investors had properties and buyers lined up, they could potentially make a lot of money. Some speculators put down a few thousand pounds and ended up with enough money to retire.

The problem is flipping and off plan investments only work in a rising market. In a sluggish or falling market, these deals have the potential to bankrupt an investor.

Developers finance their projects in stages – sometimes called *'tranches'* - based on the number of units sold.

If demand falls, the banks stop lending and the developer runs out of cash.

Should the developer go to the wall, any investor with cash tied up in the project as deposits on off plan deals can lose their money. Some investors have lost a lot of cash either completing or backing out of deals as a development completes with the home value plummeting below the buying price.

Mistake 4 - How apartment prices fell flat

City apartments are a new phenomenon in the UK. Living in flats is popular in densely populated areas where land is expensive. In Hong Kong and Tokyo, Japan, many opt to live in high-rise block because houses with gardens cost too much for many families.

Even in Britain, a homeowner would rather buy a house than an apartment for the same money or a little more because the house would come with more space and a garden.

Consequently, many flats and apartments were snapped up by property investors thinking flats are easy to maintain and straightforward to let. Modern apartment developments generally contain 30 to 50 flats in several blocks.

Chapter 2 - Avoiding Costly Property Mistakes

In a flat or deflationary period for house prices, the problem for a property investor is often the rents are low because so many landlords are vying for the same business with identical flats. The only basis for competition to differentiate one flat from another is price.

The same goes for the selling price, especially if a glut of flats comes on to the market.

Buy to let investors in this market place are struggling to break even on rents that only just cover the mortgage because the purchase was at the top of the last housing bubble.

Many of these 'luxury' apartments were overpriced by developers. New-build flats were designed to have an edge with open plan living, swish lighting and top of the market – meaning expensive – kitchen units and appliances.

The developer slapped a price tag on the apartment more often than not to reflect the lifestyle image rather than the build cost.

Then the surveyor came along to independently verify the price. Unfortunately, independence seemed to fly out of the window in many cases as the surveyor and the developer colluded to fix valuations.

Over valuations tipped the marketing balance for developers who had a built-in something extra above their margin to offer incentives.

This extra margin funded artificial discounts, cash backs, special finishes and gifted deposits.
In a rising house price market, this is great for buyers and developers. When the prices start to tumble form their peak that everyone realises their mistakes.

Chapter 2 - Avoiding Costly Property Mistakes

New-build apartments at prices that let investors secure cheap homes to build multi-million pound portfolios in double quick time as house prices soared magnified the chance to make a killing in property.

Equally, prices sinking in to a trough magnified how property investors can make a loss just a easily.

Mistake 5 - Putting lots of cash into deals

Property people always want to know whether pumping cash in to a deal or paying off a mortgage is a good idea.

The Wealth Dragon strategy is to put as little money down as possible and to always look at 'leveraging' your portfolio.

Leverage means different calculations to investors with money in various assets. Generally, leverage is the percentage value of a property tied to mortgages and other finance.

A £1 million portfolio with a total borrowing of £600,000 is leveraged at 60%.

Take this example of two investors:

- Mr A wants to invest £100,000 in stocks and shares. To buy them, he has to have ready cash available because banks will not take the risk of lending on such volatile security.

- Mr B wants to invest £100,000 in property. For a buy to let home, Mr B needs a cash deposit of £25,000 so he can arrange a mortgage for the remaining £75,000.

Both our investors complete their deals. Meanwhile, both make a £25,000 gain on their £100,000.

The gain for Mr A is 25% as he had to delve in to his savings for the entire £100,000 initial investment.

The gain for Mr B is 100% because his cash input was £25,000.

This is the power of leveraging a property investment. The potential for profits is huge for investors who can leverage no-money-down deals.

This property millionaire secret is revealed in Chapter 8.

Mistake 6 - Jumping off the property ladder

Wealth Dragons do not climb the property ladder.

Climbing the property ladder like those millionaire hopefuls on television shows who buy and fix up homes flouts Property Millionaire Secret #1: "Professional investors always make their money when they buy, not by waiting for property price inflation".

Property developers follow a different strategy. They buy in property and add value by refurbishing or redeveloping that gives the value uplift on the sale.

Uplift is a key property concept for Wealth Dragons.
Wealth Dragons create uplift when they buy. Other property people look at taking their uplift on the sale.

To clarify, Wealth Dragons may have to refurbish or develop to enhance a property to attract a better rental return. That's OK as long as the Wealth Dragon project manages and does not waste valuable time with a drill or paint brush – call in a trade.

They do the job quicker and probably to a better standard. Meanwhile, a professional investor is out looking for more deals.

Mistake 7 - Too many properties too quickly

The temptation is to buy property to build a portfolio as quickly as possible.

No money down deals let an investor buy as many properties as they like. However, having six or seven deals going through at the same time needs some managing.

The likely scenario is cash is tight as you are new to the full-time property game and out of the new acquisitions, a couple are void while undergoing light refurbishment for the first tenants and another is sitting empty waiting for tenants to move in.

That means a significant amount of potential income is lost, while the bills have to paid from somewhere.

The best way to start out is to buy a property and feel your way in to the letting process. New landlords are often unaware of the pitfalls of taking a new property to the rental market and do not build a contingency in to their budgets for delay.

Mistake 8 - Ignoring cash flow

Cash flow is important to any business, and the property business is no different. Many great businesses with poor cash flow have gone to the wall because the managers did not work to

Chapter 2 - Avoiding Costly Property Mistakes

budgets and build any contingency in to their plans.

In the recent buy to let boom, investors were known to sub-sidise rental income that failed to meet a home's outgoings. This money came from more profitable rentals from their own pockets.

Wealth Dragons would never have to do this. They crunch the numbers before completing the deal and make sure every investment is financially viable.

Building a contingency fund does not happen overnight - but something unforeseen can wipe a cash reserve out in one swoop.

Mix and match investment strategies are a good way to protect income.

For example, an investor specialising in houses and flats can look at shared houses to maximise income.

Shared houses, or houses in multiple occupation (HMOs), are the same properties let to professional couples only instead of renting the entire property to one tenant, the rooms are let as bedsits.

A three-bed house let to a family might rent for £650 a month. The same house let to four individual tenants for £75 per room per week returns £1,300 a month.

HMO landlords will agree the returns are terrific, but the downside is shared houses often need tighter hands-on man-agement than other lets plus a larger infrastructure invest-ments to meet planning and licensing restrictions.

Other ways of boosting cash flow include flipping deals or selling leads if too many opportunities are coming to a head at any one time.

Investors starting out should not give up the day job too soon. Building cash flow may take a year or more, meanwhile bills need paying.

Wealth Dragons know property investment is not so much get rich quick as stay rich for ever.

Mistake 9 - Don't stop investing

Sooner or later property investors hit a glass ceiling that leads them to reassess their strategy.

The barrier is finance, or the lack of it. Many stop investing when their cash runs out or banks and building societies refuse to lend more money.

Two factors come in to play here:

- Inactive investors do not make any money

- Just because a lender will not finance a deal does not mean the deal is not worth pursuing.

The credit crunch closing up banks and building societies for buy to let lending has led many Wealth Dragons to explore alternative financial solutions.

Two popular and profitable routes are joint ventures and lease options.

Commercial property investors have reaped the benefits of both for many years, but residential investors did not need to look at the alternatives for buy to let because funding was always available on good terms.

Now lenders have more or less shut up shop, residential investors can take the lead from their commercial colleagues about more creative financial techniques.

Joint ventures – often called *'JVs'* in the trade – are partnerships where each person brings something to the table. One partner may have the cash to finance the deal, while the other has the contacts to find investment leads and so on.

Lease options are contracts to take on a home without arranging finance. Investors profit from the cash flow without owning a property.

Mistake 10 - Waiting for the market

For many property investors, the time to buy is always now – what's happening in the market doesn't really matter as long as you follow Property Millionaire Secret#1 – Make your money when you invest.

Take the monthly charade of house price surveys – the government, banks and building societies trot out average house price statistics every month. The figures are meaningless.

No one owns an 'average' house and if an investor has made their cash going in to the deal, any gain on the back-end is a bonus.

Prices really do not matter to anyone who is not buying or selling at the time.

To an investor with a home to rent, the important statistics involve rental income and filling rental voids quickly.

By all means invest some time and effort in due diligence and check out the local prices – go online to web sites *www.rightmove.co.uk, www.hometrack.co.uk* or *www.nethouseprices.co.uk.*

These sites will give you an idea of what a property is worth and the rent a tenant will pay.

Use this information to your advantage when negotiating with a prospective seller.

Saving money with Hometrack

If you want to find out more about how Hometrack can help you accurately value your property and save thousands of pounds on renegotiating with the seller, visit *www.wealthdragons.co.uk/hometrack.htm*

Mistake 11 - Relying on one source for deals

Sensible investors spread the risk. Joint ventures were mentioned above in #9.

Sometimes investors have to play the numbers rather than play safe.

Take an investor who insists on going to the same property sourcer time after time for new deals.

The investor knows other property people are looking to the same guy for their deals, so straight away the property sourcer can up the ante and charge more on the basis someone else will take the deal if a price is not agreed.

Then this source went out of business. The investor had nowhere to go for their leads and had to waste time and money building new contacts.

Wealth Dragons do not leave their business activity to chance – they network, make contacts and spread their net widely to attract the deals they want.

Mistake 12 - Sticking to a safety zone

Everyone has a comfort zone – and for many investors that zone is sourcing property deals in specific areas.

Maybe they are near home, or somewhere they grew up and know well or just somewhere they would like to live themselves.

The reason does not matter – investors that close off possibilities are shutting the doors on deals.

Just run the numbers:

- An investor who will go the extra mile for deal that makes good money will have stacks of leads from all over.

- An investor looking at an area with a finite number of homes is restricting investment potential to just a few deals over a long period.

Wealth Dragons have an open mind about where to invest – it is the profit in the deal that makes the investment viable.

Declaration

Stand up from whatever position you're in and take a deep breath. Put your hand on your heart or point your index fingers to your temples and read out loud:

1. I will only deal with motivated sellers

2. I will not speculate on property hot spots

3. I will not speculate on new build or off-plan investments

4. I will leverage my investments by putting as little of my own money into deals as possible

5. I am a property investor, not a developer

6. I will not rush to buy too many properties too quickly

7. Cash flow is KING!

8. I'll take action now and not wait for the market

Now clench your fist and punch triumphantly in the air and say "I'm a Wealth Dragon"!

Chapter 3

Taking The Leads When Others Follow

◇◇◇

In this chapter:

- *Paying lots of interest to auctions*
- *How property finding services work*
- *Finding deals the professional way*

◇◇◇

The deals are out there for property investors - the problem is finding them.

This chapter looks at the different ways property professionals prospect for their investments. Many combine two or more of these techniques.

However they find their deals, the common factor for property professionals is they are looking for new business all the time.

Estate agents are not that special

Estate agents would like every potential home buyer and seller to believe that the only way to buy and sell a property is to beat a path to their door.

For someone looking to buy and sell a family home, estate agents offer a 'dating service' for similar homeowners looking to trade up or down.

Wealth Dragons avoid estate agents. They do not look for cosy homes but money-making investments.

Chapter 3 - Taking The Leads When Others Follow

Sellers offering their homes with an estate agent are looking for a top of the market price and are rarely motivated to sell quickly below market value.

Even if they were tempted to do a deal, the estate agent acts as a gatekeeper stifling any threat to their commission. Now and then, estate agents are offered a deal from a seller prepared to take an offer to off load a property.

These deals are few and far between. Unsurprisingly, most estate agents have a 'club' of trusted buyers who are offered first dibs at these properties – often for some sort of kick-back or commission.

Sourcing deals from estate agents requires an investment in time and effort.

That's fine if for investors who want to take that route, but most find that weighing up the input against the profit means that same time and effort is better spent elsewhere.

Two fundamental issues arise that make dealing with estate agents difficult:

- They are duty-bound to find the best price for the seller, not the buyer

- The gatekeeper problem means negotiating through the estate agent, so a property investor rarely has the opportunity to discuss the terms of a deal as well as the price with a seller.

For example, try negotiating a lease option with an estate agent who stands to gain no commission because the deal does not involve sale, even if the proposal is a good financial option for the home owner.

Property auctions stir up lots of interest

After disappointments with estate agents, many property investors make tracks for the next logical source of deals – an auction.

Auctions always attract lots of interest from all sorts of buyers. First time buyers see them as a way to climb on to the property ladder and investors are sniffing out deals.

Television programmes like 'Homes Under the Hammer' switched buyers on to the bargains and the financial disasters masquerading as profitable investments offered at auctions. Auctions are a double-edged sword. Some investors have made a fortune in the sales room, while others have lost almost everything.

Nonetheless, if you know how to work an auction, going to a sale is a great way of finding deals.

Auction catalogues

Auctioneers put together a catalogue of properties due to go under the hammer. The catalogue is generally available online and in print.

Every lot is listed, and many include a photograph and a few lines of description. Do not expect full property details like an estate agent would put together. The auctioneer visits few, if any, of the properties.

Pricing

The catalogue listing will also give a guide price for each property.

Chapter 3 - Taking The Leads When Others Follow

Do not confuse the guide price, or guide, with the reserve price. The guide is exactly that – an indication of the property price.

The reserve price or reserve is set between the buyer and the auctioneer as the minimum price the seller will accept as a bid. If the bidding fails to meet the reserve, then the property is withdrawn from sale.

Auction rooms

This is the heart and soul of the auction. Auction newbies should go on a dry run to a local sale just to see how the process works.

In an auction room, millionaires and wannabees rub shoulders and just because someone looks smart or scruffy does not mean they are what they seem.

Registered bidders have a card, generally with a number, so the auctioneer can identify them. Some bid in person and others by telephone.

Finances

Providing the reserve price is met, the highest bid wins the lot.

If you win, you need to put a 10% deposit down immediately and complete the purchase within 28 days. In the UK, auctioneers generally accept a banker's draft or cheque but not cash.

Hopefully, you solicitor is primed to deal with the contracts and searches in double-quick time.

Don't forget a home is in an auction for a good reason. In many cases, the property is deemed 'unmortgagable' because of a structural problem. Many rival bidders are in the construction trade.

Mortgage funding from a bank or building society is often too slow for buying at auction, so bridging finance is the speedier option. Often, developers have this finance lined up to buy at auctions.

Bridging finance is expensive, with interest repayments costing between 1-3% a month.

If a property needs a lot of building work to reach the standard for a mainstream mortgage, then the budget must include these interest and other finance costs, like arrangement fees.

What auction buyers need to know

The potential for profits is a big attraction – but do not forget to weigh up whether buying at auction is a sensible option.

One investor bought a property at auction without checking out the lie of the land only to discover a public right of way let anyone walk across the front garden, past the side of the house and out of the back garden to the railway station.

The moral is properties go to auction for a reason – so try and find out what it is before parting with any cash.

Vincent wanted to bid for a property at auction. The guide price was £125,000. He had a surveyor provide a valuation suggesting the market value was £185,000, which left a good margin for profit if he won the bidding.

The auctioneer called for opening bids and a voice shouted

from the back of the room: "£200,000". Vincent was aston-
ished and confused. The property was worth £15,000 less than
the bid even before spending any money on a refurbishment
and finance costs.

Why the bidder opened at £200,000 is not known, and Vincent
did not stay around to listen for the final price.

The episode gives some insight in to the way people can be-
have at auctions.

Consider paying for a survey

Paying for a survey can save thousands on a sour deal, if a
survey is not practical, at least look over the property with a
professional builder who can point out potential problems and
give some idea of the cost to put them right.

Vincent spent £400 on a survey of the property he wanted at
auction *(See above)*.

Let a lawyer loose on the title

Asking a solicitor to look up the title documents should flag potential legal issues. This is not unduly expensive as full searches are not involved, just a quick check of the title documents at
the Land Registry.

Cash flow

Buying on a bridging loan ties up equity and cash until the deal
is refinanced. Auction redevelopments are a money pit as expensive interest payments suck up savings and profits.

If the deal turns sour, the losses are huge and the consequences of possible bankruptcy will ruin an investor's property business. Having a financial cushion to soften the landing if the budget is blown out of the water is sensible.

Set a ceiling for bidding

A simple but effective tactic. Before the auction, take a minute and calculate what purchase price the deal makes sense and do not pay a penny more.

This is where due diligence with a survey and the solicitor pays dividends. Going in to an auction with a plan makes all the difference between a professional investor and a novice. A professional will have bridging finance or a mortgage lined up on the strength of researching the deal.

Winning the bidding may feel good on the day, but the real result worth having is the profit from the deal.

Before and after at an auction

Auctions are more than just a few hours of hustle and bustle on the big day. A lot of business is completed outside the sale room before and after the sale. The auctioneer wants to sell, so is open to offers.

Here's two winning strategies that can make a professional investors thousands of pounds without the need to set foot in the sale room:

- If you are keen to buy a property listed for an auction, call the sale room before auction day and ask if the seller would consider a bid.

    The trick is not to go too low. View and check for defects and try and set a fair market value for the property. Put in an offer at about 25% less than the market value.

Many sellers are happy to accept a reasonable offer without the risk of going to sale and not meeting the reserve. Make withdrawing the property from the sale a condition of the offer.

- Some professional investors win at auctions by jumping in after the sale. Here, the trick is still carrying out due diligence but instead of going head-to-head with other bidders, wait until the dust has settled

If the lot failed to meet the reserve and is withdrawn from the sale, you have a good idea of what the seller will accept. Compare the figure with what you would have offered, and if the match is reasonable, approach the auctioneer with a bid.

Both these strategies are successful for many property professionals.

Property finders are not keepers

Property finders or *'sourcers'* charge a fee for giving professional investors below market value deals.

Generally, the property finder will have negotiated the below market value deal with the owner and is selling on the package to an investor.

For example, a property is worth £100,000, but the finder negotiates a deal with the seller at £70,000, and will sell to an investor for £80,000. The investor is buying at 20% below market value but the finder is charging £10,000 at the back end. Often, the investor has no idea of the price agreed with the seller. It's like buying from a shop. The customer pays a price, maybe even in a sale, but rarely knows the wholesale cost of the goods to the retailer. That's the back end.

Front end fees are more transparent. The finder tells the investor a property is worth £100,000 but the agreed sale price is £70,000.

That's a healthy 30% below market value. The finder generally charges 2%-3% of the property valuation or the purchase price of the property.

Different property sourcers have their own terms of business. Some sell 'packaged' or ready made' deals that can include finding a mortgage lender, completing the loan applications and instructing solicitors.

Property business sales and marketing

Professional investors want to sit in front of as many motivated sellers as they can find because agreeing a deal is as much about settling on the terms as a price.

To find motivated sellers, investors need to understand and apply sales and marketing skills.

Many new investors find selling themselves to prospective customers a daunting task.

They try and avoid the issue or settle on buying leads or packaged deals because despite the cost, it's easier.

Top professional investors are also slick sales and marketing machines. One of the key attributes separating those at the top of their game and the rest are these skills. Most investors give up before they start selling. Just hold these thoughts for a while.

When Vincent started his property business, he hated picking up the phone and talking to customers.

Like most investors, he thought he could not sell but he figured out everyone was born with the skills. The proof is children negotiating with their mums and dads every day... and generally getting their own way.

Marketing is about reaching out to sellers and finding common ground with a message that provokes them in to making contact.

Sellers need a reason to speak to you, so give them what they want. Tell them that:

- You can complete quickly

- You can offer solutions and flexible terms

- You understand their circumstances

If you have noticed the tone has changed from talking about investors to what you can offer.

Sales are about personal relationships, about communicating with strangers and making them feel comfortable about dealing with you.

Negotiation is a life-skill that is called in to action every day, whether you are dealing with your boss, colleagues or shopping for a bargain, if you cannot negotiate or influence others, then others will influence you. For more about negotiation, see Chapter 10.

The Internet

Here's a Wealth Dragons secret revealed – all the leads sold on our web site come directly from the internet. In three years, the Wealth Dragons have generated more than 40,000 leads from homeowners who want to sell quickly.

For more about sourcing low-cost property leads online, see Chapter 11.

Advertising and Leafleting

Close behind the internet for sourcing property leads comes the old-school print media – newspapers and leaflets.

Property professionals find deals from newspaper advertisements.

Others make a good living from leaflets. Depending on where you live, you may well have seen leaflets asking questions like 'Do you want to sell quickly for cash?', 'Facing repossession?' or 'Quick completion?'

Buying Leads

Property investors can search and buy leads at the Wealth Dragons web site *www.networkpropertyinvestment.co.uk*.

A lead is contact information from a motivated seller. Sellers regularly leave their contact details on the web site. Property investors can buy these leads from about £25 to £125 each. Buying the lead lets you deal directly with the seller – but that does not guarantee a deal. That is down to your negotiating skill.

Converting leads to deals is a numbers game. The better you can negotiate, the more leads you will convert in to deals.

Other Creative Methods

Different property investors feel comfortable selling and marketing their own niches. Some put banners up in supermarkets. Others like to press the flesh and walk an area chatting to people with local knowledge, like the postie or window cleaner, who both meet lots of people every day.

For the Wealth Dragons, the internet works, although we have tried lots of other methods along the way. There's no real right and wrong – marketing is just a tool to bring in leads.

Declaration

Stand up from whatever position you're in and take a deep breath.

Put your hand on your heart or point your index fingers to your temples and read out loud:

1. **I know lots of ways to find property deals**

2. **Sales and marketing skills have everything to do with successful property investment**

3. **I will excel at sales and marketing**

Now clench your fist and punch triumphantly in the air and say "I'm a Wealth Dragon"!

Chapter 4

Rich Pickings
For Cash Buyers

◇◇

In this chapter:

- *Becoming a cash buyer*
- *Why sellers need a cash buyer*
- *Understanding bridging finance*

◇◇

Cash buyers, contrary to popular belief, do not have wads of money brimming out of their wallets and are unlikely to have a lot of zeros after their bank balance.

Even if they did, it's unlikely someone who had the financial ability to build a fortune would risk their own cash in a couple of property deals.

The likelihood of a buyer coming along with a briefcase full of cash is slim, to say the least. The chance it's a Wealth Dragon is even slimmer as they follow the rule of putting little of their own money down to finance an investment.

Nevertheless, shattering a seller's illusion of an investor's ability to solve their problems is not good.

Playing the role of a cash buyer

Professional investors know that a cash buyer is really just someone with the resources to quickly close a deal. Those resources do not necessarily belong to them – they are often borrowed.

Chapter 4 - Rich Pickings For Cash Buyers

All you really have to do is come across as their image of a cash buyer.

That's what professional investing is about. You don't have to have lots of money in the bank to become a cash buyer, but you do have to demonstrate the right characteristics:

Paying the seller's legal fees

A flexible term to make selling more affordable for someone who is in financial difficulty. Buying their home direct saves them estate agents costs, and in the scheme of £100,000 plus deals, a few hundred pounds out of your pocket is not going to break the bank, but gives the seller an incentive to do business.

Putting money where your mouth is

Lots of investors can talk a good deal, but professional investors are hot to trot with finance and a deposit in place. Showing you already have bridging or a mortgage in place proves you can complete quicker than someone who may make a better offer but is not ready to move.

Breaking the sales chain

Cash buyers say they can complete in 28 days - and often do. As an independent buyer with no property to sell to finalise the deal, the seller is not waiting for the rest of the chain to move so they can complete.

Flexible terms

This is where dealing direct is so important. Cutting out a middleman means you can address the seller's personal issues by tailoring the deal to their personal financial circumstances. Offering flexible options is like lenders offering different mortgages.

The mortgage is still a mortgage but the package is adjusted for the needs of different buyers – think fixed rate, cash back and tracker. In most cases, the incentive is the same but delivered on the front end, the back end or over a specified time.

Why become a cash buyer?

Investing as a cash buyer is a matter of perception – for the seller. The perception of a cash buyer offers several advantages in the seller's eyes. These advantages are also a benefit to the buyer because they let you bring added-value to the deal.

This added value does not come free, but allows you to negotiate more favourable terms. So, here's some examples of how this added value can work:

Speed – No one minds paying a little extra for convenience, quick delivery and better service. Cash buyers can command a discount on the house price because they can complete fast.

Certainty – Sellers want a guarantee their property is sold and they will have an agreed amount of cash in their hand on a specific date. Someone who cannot deliver because they have to arrange finance or wait for a chain cannot deliver the goods like a cash buyer. Like speed, guaranteed performance comes at a price.

On the streets where unmotivated sellers live, house purchases are negotiated differently from those where motivated sellers are itching to leave.

Chapter 4 - Rich Pickings For Cash Buyers

Unmotivated sellers have time and can afford to sit and wait for the best price. They make the pitch: 'This house is worth £100,000, make me your best offer.'

Not everyone has time to wait and many motivated sellers surprisingly just want quick cash.

The Wealth Dragons often meet sellers who say: "Look, I've had this house left to me and it's worth £100,000. I don't really need all that money. I just want £20,000 now so I don't have to work and can take a year or two off so I can travel."

Who needs a cash buyer?

As we discussed above, unmotivated sellers who have the time, patience and money to wait for the right price are not the target market of professional property investors.

Professional investors need to speak to people who want quick cash – and some of the major sources of these leads are:

Debt problems

Up to 35 leads a day come from sellers in financial difficulty – often with credit card and loan companies.
The Wealth Dragons have seen some unscrupulous mortgage companies charging interest rates up to 20% on mortgages.

Sellers often want solutions to stop repossession. Some borrowers secure loans on their homes in the good financial times and spend the cash on luxuries, like holidays and cars.

Then the bad times hit and the main earner loses their job and can't afford to meet the repayments leading to the lender to take action to repossess the home.

Chapter 4 - Rich Pickings For Cash Buyers

Divorce

Couples and marriages are forever moving in together then splitting. About 85% of those coming to the Wealth Dragons for help want to sell for emotional reasons. They just want to sell quickly for closure on an unpleasant time in their lives.

Stuck in a Chain

About a third of all house sales fall through for one reason or another, and if a seller is above or below one of these unfortunate transactions in the chain, then they may lose their buyer and have to return to square one and start again.

The classic deal is to negotiate with everyone in the chain to absorb the costs of someone moving at a below-market-value price so everyone is standing a little pain for the rest of the team but everyone can move on.

Moving Overseas

A good number of people have an eye on their place in the sun and fear they will lose their dream home if they cannot put in an offer and move quickly. Professional property investors can solve this problem with a quick cash sale.

Inheritance

Many inherited properties are outdated and cost money to modernise before they command a good price on the market. The sellers are often relatives who live away from the area and do not have the inclination to refurbish and manage property.

Cash buyers can solve the problem and as a family, no one loses too much with a below-market-value deal.

How can you become a cash buyer?

It's important that you work with the right team, just as it's important for you to be around other professionals that can deliver your guarantees. Your reputation and pocket suffers if mortgages and the legals are not completed on time, not those of your team.

Brokers and lawyers

Pick a financial and legal team who can move fast, like mortgage brokers who have good connections with lenders and lawyers who can telescope the typical 12 week conveyance in to 28 days.

By team, select more than one mortgage broker and lawyer.

That way, your deals are not held up by holidays, problems or workloads. Every transaction needs two lawyers – one for the buyer and another for the seller. To avoid delay and other complications, make sure the lawyers are on the approved lists of your lenders.

One other issue is family solicitors often misunderstand how a cash deal works because they are unfamiliar with the transaction. They tend to persuade their clients not to deal with cash buyers because they view "creative solutions" as unethical.

There are two main reasons for this way of thinking:

1. They don't understand cash buyers and the quick sale process

2. They fail to consider the seller's personal circumstances

If a seller wishes to employ their own family solicitor, then "pre-frame" them by explaining their solicitor could advise against the transaction and give them the reasons.

A point to make is – "would you employ a divorce lawyer to deal with your compensation injury claim?" Of course you wouldn't.

Crossing the bridging finance problem

Cash buyers either have a deposit to hand or work with a bridging firm on no money down deals.

Bridging finance is straightforward. For example, if you buy a house right now, you have need a deposit and mortgage. If the property is worth £100,000, the lender might advance £70,000 if you pay a deposit of £30,000.

If you do not have a deposit, then you can borrow bridging finance.

More about picking a winning property team – *See Chapter 6.*

How bridging finance works

As a simple rule, if you buy a property right now between 25% and 30% below the market value, you won't have to put any money into the deal.

You need to go to a bridging financier with a deal with 25-35% negotiated off the price of the property.

The bridger will lend the deposit by putting a charge on other property in the investor's portfolio, providing sufficient equity is available.

Chapter 4 - Rich Pickings For Cash Buyers

This is how the deal works:

Property valuation:	£100,000
Seller accepts:	£70,000 (30% below market value)
Bank loans:	£52,500 (75% of £70,000)
Bridging finance:	£17,500 (Bank needs to see deposit)

The property is then refinanced, based on a full market value of £75,000 (75% of £100,000). Most banks will not refinance until at least six months after buying or taking out a mortgage.

Out of the £75,000, the £52,000 loan is repaid, giving a cash back of £23,000. If the bridging finance interest is 1% per month for six months, the cost for the bridging is £1,050, giving a net cash back of £21,950. Don't forget to factor in other costs, like legal fees to give a net cash back.

Not bad for 6 months work for one property deal!

Declaration

Stand up from whatever position you're in and take a deep breath. Put your hand on your heart or point your index fingers to your temples and read out loud:

1. **I am a cash buyer who can help sellers move quickly**

2. **I am resourceful and have more than one way of helping sellers depending on their situations**

3. **I have a winning team that can move quickly and efficiently**

Now clench your fist and punch triumphantly in the air and say "I'm a Wealth Dragon"!

Chapter 5

Copy writing - Your Silent Salesman

Copy writing is a silent salesman that speaks volumes about you and your property business.

Sharp copy writing is a skill that separates property professionals from the rest.

Many articulate and persuasive speakers face a mental block when trying to put the words that flow in conversation down on paper. These speakers only find copy writing difficult because they try and change their style when writing.

The secret of good copy writing is simply writing as if you were having a conversation. When you speak, you automatically order the facts to make what you say interesting, with the most important information first.

That's all copy writing is – putting your words and thoughts on paper or on screen.

Grabbing attention with words

Everywhere you look, you will see marketing material trying

to grab your attention. Just look around a restaurant, pub or bar. You will see menus, posters, leaflets, match books and beer mats.

Online, web sites are crammed with classified and banner ads, articles and widgets all trying to catch your eye. What you have to do is work out who you want to read your web pages, leaflets or adverts and phrase them in a way that will capture their attention.

Writing online or offline is no different, the skills and principles are the same. Just remember the smaller the space and the fewer the words, the harder it becomes to put across your message.

Writing a 300 word article for a newspaper or web site about copy writing skills is a lot easier than attracting attention with just 10 or 12 well chosen words with Google Adwords.

A good resource that explains how people read web pages is Jakob Nielson's site at www.useit.com.

His team analysed thousands of web pages to conclude readers only spend a few seconds reading copy and few read more than 300 words when they visit a web site.

His research also shows that readers scan a page in an 'F' pattern rather than read every word and quickly move on if they find nothing of interest to attract their attention.

Why copy writing is important

Copy writing, marketing and sales are linked skills.

Copy writing puts your message out – and marketing is the

means of reaching your potential customers. Good marketing targeting the right audience creates leads. Converting leads gives sales and sales lead to profits.

Without profits, you have no business, so the trick here is to match marketing activity to give you the number of leads that you can convert in to the level of sales you want.

No marketing means no sales, which in turn means no profits. Your business cannot afford to neglect marketing.

If you do not market, you still need leads to convert to sales – and that's where packagers and lead-selling sites like the Wealth Dragon's www.networkpropertyinvestment.co.uk come in to prop your business while you work on kicking in your own marketing.

Cutting through information overload

It's a wonder our heads don't explode with the information overload we are subjected to all day every day from marketing.

Wherever you go, someone is trying to sell, up sell, cross sell and sell again. You should also assume you are not the only professional property investor working whatever patch or niche you decide is right for you.

So what makes that prospective motivated seller respond to your online message, leaflet or newspaper advert? The answer is the marketing message in your copy.

Swiping inspiration from all around

Swipe files are a tool of the trade for copywriters. They are always assimilating information, soaking up other people's ideas and turn of phrase like sponges.

Swipe files are like those picture boards interior designers put together for clients - but instead of fancy furnishings and collections of colour, these files are bits of leaflet, web site screen dumps or clippings torn from magazines.

If someone has an idea or design you like, do not copy but develop the idea to suit your needs.

AIDA to the rescue

As the comedian Frank Carson says, it's the way you tell 'em – and that stands good for copy writing as well as stand-up comedy.

Copy writing is not just a mass of words that looks pretty – it's a considered and linked web that draws the reader in to find out more.

Some copywriters follow AIDA – the acronym for the four stages of the sales process. It's not perfect, but it's as good as any other formula for writing. After a while, you'll find you write naturally without having to think about a formula.

AIDA stands for Attention, Interest, Desire and Action.

Attention

Headlines are a short title that grabs the reader and alert them to content that is of interest.

Headlines are a good place to remind copywriters of an important rule – do not write in the passive mood.

Chapter 5 - Copy writing - Your Silent Salesman

Unravel what this means and you will understand: *This topic can cause major problems for copywriters, but it shouldn't*

The sentence should read: *Copywriters should not have major problems with this topic*

The first is written in the passive mood, and the second in the active mood.

Verbs – doing words – are active when the subject is carrying out the action of the verb, like 'Fred ran across the road'. Fred is doing the running.

They are passive when the when the subject is having the action of the verb carried out on it, like 'the road was crossed by Fred'.

Active writing is punchy, sharp and to the point. Passive is not.

'Cash paid for your home' is good

'Sell your home in 28 days' is better than *'How to Sell Your House in 2 Weeks!'*

The second phrase has too many wasted words in front of the meat of the sentence.

'Stop repossession' is positive and to the point, while good copywriters avoid questions like *'Facing repossession?'*

The last point to avoid is overusing an exclamation mark (!) – great writers like Mark Twain, author of Tom Sawyer, claim this is the hallmark of a lazy writer.

Lastly, never make promises you cannot keep in a headline or copy.

Chapter 5 - Copy writing - Your Silent Salesman

Interest

Once your headline has grabbed attention, the reader will scan your opening line or the 'intro' before reading on. The intro is a summary of the rest of the story in 30 words or less. Too short and the reader will move on, while too long and they will lose concentration.

'Sell Your Home in 28 Days
Sell your home in 28 days to a cash buyer – guaranteed. Call 0123 456789 or visit www.mywebsite.co.uk now for more details'

In 22 words, your copy has answered all the prospective seller's main questions –

Who? – A cash buyer is ready and waiting

Why? – Because the cash buyer can solve your financial problem right now

Where? – Just call the number or go to the web site

What? – It's a service that stops repossession

When? – Within 14 days guaranteed

Of course, you can write some more sentences to expand on the intro, ending with another 'call to action' – a short sentence telling the reader to contact your business. For example, how many businesses exploit the call to action as a discount voucher or 'while stocks last' offer.

Desire

Most people do not like make life-changing decisions unless

they have to. Motivation and opportunity lead to decision making – which neatly takes us back to wanting to sit in front of motivated sellers.

Motivated sellers want a solution and generally, an easy way out of their predicament. It's human nature.

Your copy writing job is to point out what will happen if they do not act –and how you can help them through the process to find a solution to their problem.

Action

Once you have grabbed that potential lead's attention and prompted them to wanting to contact you, don't forget to put a clear and concise call to action on all your marketing material. It seems obvious but it's an easy point to overlook.

Take the DIY firm that took a full page colour advert in a big city local paper to promote a massive money saving special offer – and then forgot to put their business name and contact details on the ad.

Don't fall in to the same trap.

Testing and measuring

That 'Quote reference ABC' tag on a leaflet or advert is carefully placed for a reason – so advertisers can measure the effectiveness of their marketing.

Some leaflet drops have calls to action like "Call Jane" or "quote reference #ABC". In reality, Jane and the reference number are just to identify the batch or source of the advertising when the prospect calls up so you may measure the performance.

Chapter 5 - Copy writing - Your Silent Salesman

A-B testing is another tried and tested marketing strategy. An advertiser will run two ads in the same publication – one in week 1 and the other in week 2.

The ads will be different and the response to each collated. If one turns out to trigger more interest than the other, then the successful ad will run again while the other is dropped.

Google run a similar strategy on their advertising programs.

Declaration

Stand up from whatever position you're in and take a deep breath. Put your hand on your heart or point your index fingers to your temples and read out loud:

1. **Being successful is doing what the majority of people are reluctant to do**

2. **Copy writing is important and I will master it to become successful**

3. **I need to create desire first before closing a sale**

4. **I'll start a swipe file now (go and find a folder)**

Now clench your fist and punch triumphantly in the air and say "I'm a Wealth Dragons"!

Chapter 6

Picking A Winning Property Team

<><><><><><><><><><><><><><><><><><><><><><><><><><><><><><>

In this chapter:

- *Who you need on your side*
- *Looking for help from other investors*
- *Moving forward with a mentor to guide the way*

<><><><><><><><><><><><><><><><><><><><><><><><><><><><><><>

Professional property investors are like captains of a ship. They may steer the vessel from the bridge, but they are reliant on other professionals to keep the ship on course, just like the captain has his officers, engineers and crew.

In Chapter 4, you saw the property professional's team needs to have more than one expert for each position, to cover for holidays, illness and other unforeseen problems.

Who do you need on your side?

It's sensible to pick team members who do not know each other, so you can reveal as much or as little as you wish about your business. So who do you need on your team?

Lawyers

This is a key role – you need lawyers who will fast track your deals.

Most purchases will need two lawyers – one acting for you and the other acting for the seller.

Chapter 6 - Picking A Winning Property Team

Your solicitor will need to have some experience in completing no-money down and bridging deals.

The job of the solicitor acting for a buyer is to ensure no legal conflicts of interest arise and to handle the conveyancing. Conveyancing is the legal procedure involving the transfer of title to a property from one person to another.

This involves requesting reports on the property from the local council relating to any planning issues, and finding out if the property is liable to flooding or near an old mine. Searches will also highlight any rights of way other people might have over your land.

A legal specialist may have to advise on lease options.

Although it's true most solicitors are conveyancers, not all of them have enough cases crossing their desks to be experts concerning every issue that may arise.

Some people call solicitors 'deal killers' – some are good but others are less so. Find lawyers who understand professional property investment, not just normal home conveyancing. One tip is you need lawyers who return calls and give your enquiries priority.

If a lawyer won't give you the time or sounds abrupt, then you wouldn't want to work with them anyway, so move on.

Accountant and tax specialist

Accountants are doubly important to property investors.

First, the administration involved in running a property business is complicated and time-consuming for any portfolio of more than a couple of properties. Keeping neat records and handing them to an accountant frees up time while making sure forms are filed and deadlines are met.

A good property accountant will also know what business expenses you can and cannot claim and how to present the information to a tax inspector.

Your accountant should advise on business structure - for instance if you are buying and letting residential property, that is one business, and perhaps 'flipping' property – buying and selling quickly at a profit - now and then as well, which is a separate business that requires separate accounts and record-keeping.

In this case, you may well run your property investment business as a sole trader but your 'flipping' business as a limited company

Next, an accountant will help with complex tax issues like helping you pay less capital gains tax when you sell an investment property.

Builders and tradesmen

Builders - most people cannot live with them – but property professionals cannot function without them.

You need a builder you can trust to manage your projects for you. Your builder needs to bring the job in on time and to budget.

Good builders can keep costs down and boost profits. For example, Nicola had to set a floating floor in a property conversion to comply with building regulations.

The architect had a specific procedure in mind that involved a layer of double insulation wool, a second layer of flooring, and slab insulation on top.

The builder looked at the plans and said he knew another way to lay the floor that would pass building regulations. He discussed the proposal with the building inspector, who passed the plan. His intervention saved time and several thousand in costs.

The right builder saves time, stress and money. Nicola's first refurbishment cost £26,000, yet she could deliver the same refurbishment now for £7,000 with the right builder.

An advanced strategy is partnering with a trusted builder to sell a property that is turning in to a money pit. John's builder fixed up a property at his own cost, then shared the profits from the resulting rental. When the property sold, they simply split the profit.

Bridger

Bridging is short-term finance that secures a property for no money down deals, as discussed in Chapter 4.

Mortgage broker

An independent mortgage broker is someone who has access to all mortgage providers.

At any one time, hundreds of lenders are offering lots of mortgage products at different rates and terms.

A mortgage broker can advise the best borrowing options for each deal. Valuations are often arranged through mortgage brokers. The amount you can borrow depends on the survey.

Chapter 6 - Picking A Winning Property Team

If the valuation comes back below the expected price, a good mortgage broker can appeal to the surveyor to revise his report.

Mortgage brokers can give a lending "decision in principle" (DIP) within minutes That gives an idea of how much the lender will advance and the likely terms and costs. Do not forget a DIP is no guarantee that the lender won't change their mind.

Mortgage brokers charge a typical fee of 1% of the loan. Some may agree a fixed fee if you place a high volume of deals with them.

Letting and managing agents

Letting agents find tenants and manage property. They work on a 'let only' or full management basis.

Before buying, letting agents can give a good indication of the rental a property will achieve and the demand for that type of property in the local market.

After buying, they can find tenants, collect the rent and deal with day-to-day matters like small repairs.

Graphics designers and web developers

Designing marketing materials and web sites is time-consuming. Like finding a builder, deal with a professional you can trust and get along with and let them do the work for you.

That way, you have consistent business branding and someone available to revise leaflets, letters and web pages as and when you need them. Sourcing leads from a web site is only part of an online marketing campaign. You will most likely need to manage tools like Google pay per click advertising.

Looking for help from other investors

A cash-rich investor is usually someone who doesn't have much time but plenty of money.

They don't want to go out and do the work – they want other people to do the work with them for a share of the profit. These are the typical armchair investors.

If you want to make money from deals you've agreed, you could charge investors between £3,000 and £10,000 per deal.

For example, if you have agreed a deal where the net profit from the rental per month is £300, then the rental per year is £3,600. A cash investment of £5,000 from an investor could yield a return of £3,600 x 100/ £5,000 = 72% per year.

A cash-rich investor might also fund your marketing. When John first started in property, he had a cash-rich investor in-putting £2,000 a month so he could free up his time and become a full-time property professional.

A cash-rich investor is an invaluable ally.

Time-rich investors

Time-rich investors are generally newbies who want a full-time property career; for instance, they may have given up work or lost their job and want to learn about property investment.

You can trade knowledge for their time. Teach them what you've learned from this course, and in return they can take on time-consuming jobs for you.

Joint venture partners

This is a prime example of where you can speed up your investing. Joint venture partners come in four main types -

- Time-rich, cash-poor

- Cash-rich, time-poor

- Knowledge-rich, cash-poor

- Cash-rich, knowledge poor

To create an ideal partnership, you need to find someone who fills a gap by complementing your skills.

For instance, two cash-rich partners in business together does not make best use of their skills or attributes.

Moving forward with a mentor

A mentor is someone who can guide you and fast-track your success. By working with a mentor, you are putting yourself in the position of a time-rich investor.

When you choose a mentor, make sure they understand the modelling process.

If it's taken the mentor four years to learn something, the modelling process will allow the learner to learn it in a fraction of the time.

The Wealth Dragons have an apprenticeship that coaches students to take action on an on-going basis. To find out more information, call +44 (0)1908 698873.

Chapter 6 - Picking A Winning Property Team

Declaration

Stand up from whatever position you're in and take a deep breath. Put your hand on your heart or point your index fingers to your temples and read out loud:

1. I will build a winning team

2. I need to find a mentor to help my education

Now clench your fist and punch triumphantly in the air and say "I'm a Wealth Dragon"!

Chapter 7

Putting A Price On Property

◇◇

In this chapter:

- *Don't ignore your due diligence*
- *Valuing a property*
- *Calculating the returns on rent*

◇◇

Almost every day TV, radio and the papers carry stories about the rise and fall of house prices. How prices perform is fast catching up with the weather as a favourite topic of conversation.

The problem with all these house price watchers is none of them can give an accurate price for a specific property – the figures are all worked out for an average house.

Guesstimates of house prices are not good enough for property professionals. Anyone making a business decision that could bankrupt them if the deal goes wrong can afford to make a mistake.

That's why taking care to carry out 'due diligence' is so important to a Wealth Dragon.

What is due diligence?

Due diligence is the jargon for the duty of an investor to gather information on any likely risks involved in a property transaction.

Chapter 7 - Putting A Price On Property

Breaking that down, before parting with any money, an investor should take all reasonable steps to answer three key questions:

- How much would the property make sold on the open market?

- How much rent is a tenant likely to pay

- How much will refurbishing the property to a suitable standard to let cost?

Why is due diligence important?

Think of a property deal as a boxing ring – due diligence is the ropes that set the area where you fight.

The way you structure the deal is the ring. As long as you stay in the ropes, where you stand and what you do doesn't really matter.

The financial parameters of a property deal are set by due diligence. You can change the purchase price, pay legal fees or offer cash back. As long as you agree a deal within the parameters set by due diligence, you will make a profit.

Failing to complete satisfactory due diligence means your deal has no boundaries, so the negotiations can end up anywhere, even in the red.

Due diligence step-by-step

Effective due diligence underpins the success of every property deal.

Chapter 7 - Putting A Price On Property

The old legal saying *'caveat emptor'* comes in to play – it means *'buyer beware'*. The phrase came about for a meaning and is a warning not to take anything a seller, valuer or lender says at face value because they all have their own agendas.

Your best way to approach due diligence is to have an assessment process for qualifying each deal.

Qualifying motivated sellers is looked at in Chapter 10, next here's some tips and advice for due diligence:

Valuing a property

This is the first due diligence question. Inexperienced investors often pay too much for a property because they take someone's word for how much a property is worth.

Don't forget the price a seller wants to achieve is the asking price and has no relevance in your due diligence.

You want to know how much the property will reasonably value because this sets two parameters in the deal:

- The market value gives you a figure to discount for agreeing a purchase price

- The market value gives you the starting point for calculating how much a lender will advance when you remortgage the property

Any surveyor valuing the property will look at the selling prices of three similar properties within 800 metres during the past six months. If no matching properties are found, then the search area is widened and the time period extended. You should look for the same 'comparables' as the surveyor. Often, a surveyor will approach local estate agents for comparables, but you can also search online.

Several official and unofficial sites log this data – the Land Registry (*www.landregistry.gov.uk*) list sold property data but can be three months out of date.

Other sites take the Land Registry data for free access online –

Mouseprice (*www.mouseprice.com*) is one that links in to other neighbourhood data, like school rankings, crime statistics and the like.

Hometrack (*www.hometrack.co.uk)* or Net House Prices (*www.nethouseprices.co.uk*), and Rightmove (*www.rightmove.co.uk*) also take the Land Registry data feed for free online searching.

Be careful with other price watch surveys, like the Nationwide and Halifax.

Their figures are based on mortgage applications and approvals, not sealed deals, so the figures returned are unreliable as valuations.

If you want to find out more about how Hometrack can help you accurately value your property and save thousands of pounds on renegotiating with the seller visit *http://www.wealthdragons.co.uk/hometrack.htm*

How surveyors manipulate prices

When checking a market value, remember that even if a comparable property sold for £X recently, if the current "asking price" for the property you are checking, or another similar one, is on the market with an estate agent for a lower price, then the surveyor will probably come back with a figure lower than £X. The reason is the surveyor normally has a notion that a property is worth as much as whatever someone is willing to pay.

The valuer's logic is that even though a similar property sold for more recently, if a seller is willing to accept a lower price now, then other properties are worth less as well.

Here are some valuation examples:

Down valuing to the asking price

If a property is on the market with an estate agent for £120,000, you may find that from your research, a similar property with the same condition was sold a few months ago for £140,000.

In theory, your property is also worth £140,000.

However, the surveyor would use the £120,000 "asking price" as the benchmark and discount from there because few properties achieve their "asking prices".

In these circumstances, expect a valuation between £110,000 and £120,000. A prudent investor would expect a valuation of around £110,000. Any higher figure is a bonus.

Down valuing to the offer price

Taking £120,000 from the example above as a starting point, if the valuer finds out from the seller that the "actual" sale price is below market value, say £95,000, then the report will show that the property is only "worth as much as it is offered".

For either of these deals work, the property valuation has to reflect the open market value and not the purchase price.

Chapter 7 - Putting A Price On Property

Most surveyors may down value a property if the purchase price is disclosed. These examples are based on surveys carried out for Wealth Dragons.

They are by no means indicative of how your own valuations would transpire because valuation is, after all, an art.

If you try to "tap into a surveyor's mind" by following their typical ways of thinking as illustrated in the examples above, you may achieve much better results.

How much will a lender give on a valuation?

This is the million dollar question. First, you need to think of financing a project in terms of a two step transaction.

First, finance the purchase, generally with the help of a bridging loan or cash-rich partner to secure ownership.

Next, remortgage with a bank or building society to release the uplift in equity.

The second step is where the valuation report plays a more crucial part. The principle is the property is only worth the cash a buyer pays.

This principle shackles a Wealth Dragon because, as a professional investor, a Wealth Dragon always looks to buy below market value.

Don't spring the loan-to-value trap

In the UK, a mortgage lender will agree to advance funds on a percentage of the valuation or the purchase price, whichever is the lowest. This is the loan-to-value or LTV. If you agree to buy a home valued at £100,000 for the below-market-value price of £75,000, then a bank or building society is likely lend 75% on the purchase price - 75% of £75,000 is £56,250.

As an investor you're stuck with funding a deposit of £18,750, legal fees and any other cash needed to complete the deal.

You will also have to wait six months before any lender would consider a revaluation and remortgage to draw down any equity in the property. Equity is the difference between the valuation and the total borrowed against the property.

The remortgage is based on the property valuation once the first six month's have passed.

If the market valuation is £100,000, then the remortgage amount is 75% LTV or £75,000, less the initial funding of £56,250, giving an £18,750 cash back that refunds the deposit.

Financing deals this way restricts professional investment because lending rules slow down how and when properties are remortgaged to release equity.

The answer is to employ more creative financing.

Going under is the best way to value

Denial is the major problem for newbie investors. Invariably, a new investor will assume a property value that is higher than a realistic open market sale price.

This goes back to what was discussed in an earlier chapter about estate agents and asking prices *(See Chapter 3)*. Professional investors are more conservative and prudent with their valuations. The credit crunch has brought about a sea-change in valuations. Many lenders have an aggressive policy of pursuing losses on repossessed property values in the courts against valuers.

Now, surveyors are coy in their pricing to avoid potential litigation.

A valuation in the current financial climate is more likely to err on the side of caution rather than expectation.

Professional property investors should take a more pessimistic view and strip away the denial when assessing a deal. If the value is marked down, then that's not a problem because your figures are worked for that eventuality – and if the value comes back above your assessment, then that's just more profit.

How much rent will a tenant pay?

Rental income is cash flow for your property business.

Knowing how much rent to expect from a tenant sets the parameter for how much cash is available from the deal to service day-to-day business expenses like the mortgage, insurance and any maintenance.

The rental assessment is also an integral part of any lender's calculation. Most lenders expect a property investment to self-finance – that means the investor should not input any cash subsidy to pay the mortgage.

Rent cover defined

A buy-to-let mortgage application and valuation report includes a rental assessment. The assessment is the base figure for calculating rent cover. Rent cover is an amount the lender requires to see coming in to pay the mortgage. Rent cover terms vary between lenders.

Rent cover is expressed as a percentage like 125% or 130%. This means the lender expects the property to achieve a rent that is 25% or 30% more than the monthly mortgage interest repayment.

For example, if the mortgage repayment is £220 per month, the rent cover at 125% is:

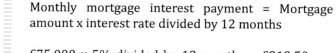

Mortgage payment:	£220
Plus 25% of the mortgage repayment:	£55
Total monthly rent cover required:	£275

So the lender would expect to see a monthly rent of at least £275 on the rental assessment.

Here's another example of how a rental assessment affects what you can borrow:

A property's market valuation is £100,000, and a 75% LTV mortgage means the lender would lend £75,000. If the mortgage interest rate is 5%, the monthly interest payment is calculated as:

Monthly mortgage interest payment = Mortgage amount x interest rate divided by 12 months

£75,000 x 5% divided by 12 months = £312.50 per month

If the mortgage lender has a rent cover of 125%, that means

the surveyor has to assess the monthly achievable rental for this property as £312.50 x 125% = £390.62

> Rental cover = Monthly mortgage interest payment x Rental cover%

Rental assessment is less than rent cover

If the rental assessment comes back at £375, the mortgage lender will cap the loan at the amount serviced by the rent cover at 125%.

This is the same calculation as above backwards:

> £375 x 12 = £4,500 as the annual rent due at 125% rent cover.
>
> To work out the mortgage loan this would service, calculate the monthly mortgage payment less the 25% rent cover:
>
> £4500 divided by 125 times 100 = £3,600
>
> At a 5% mortgage interest rate, £3,600 represents a loan of £3,600 divided by 5 x 100 = £72,000

Rental assessment more than rent cover

The lender will revert to the maximum loan-to-value for and rental assessment exceeding the required rent cover.

The basic rule of rent cover is the lender can cap the loan if the rent cover does not meet the rental assessment.

This will only offer the maximum loan-to-value if the rent cover exceeds the rental assessment.

Rental assessment due diligence

Unfortunately, no web site exists for rents along the lines of the Land Registry for sale prices.

You can track down comparables for properties advertised to let.

Google Property Maps and the usual suspects, like Rightmove and other large property portals let you search properties to let by postcode area.

An online search will also let you gauge the popularity of a property or area by showing how many similar properties are available.

If several comparables are available, this could mean the area has a lot of available property or is unpopular with renters. Both of these reasons drive down the rental assessment.

Another way of checking out the likely rental return is talking with one or two local letting agents. Just call and say you are looking at a property as an investor.

Give the name of the street, but do not identify the property. Tell them you intend to offer the property to let and give details like parking, bedrooms and the level of finish.

Ask about their management costs, how quickly they would expect to let and what they would expect as a reasonable monthly rental.

Many letting agents will put this assessment in writing. If the valuer's assessment is less than their opinions, you can send these letters to the valuer to ask for a review of the report.

How much will refurbishing to let cost?

Knowledge is power, so find out all you can about a property before you buy so you do not have any nasty, expensive surprises later on. You need to factor extra costs for refurbishing the property to let in to your due diligence.

Some properties are inherently more expensive to maintain than others due to their location or because spending decisions are in the hands of a third party like a freeholder.

Typical risks that should flag warning signals to investigate are:

Older properties

If your property is listed or stands in a conservation area, the local planning authority may have special powers that regulate how an owner can change or refurbish a property.

Typically, these restrictions would involve controlling the look of an area by specifying materials – for instance, replacement windows and doors may mean installing wooden units painted certain colours instead of white Upvc.

Check with the local planning department whether any special conditions may apply – and if so, how they may effect your plans for the property.

Leasehold properties

Most flats and maisonettes are leasehold. For example, a freeholder will own a block of apartments and licence occupation of separate flats to leaseholders for a specific length of time, like 125 years.

The leaseholders than pay the freeholder services charges and ground rent to cover the management costs of the block.

As and when repairs come due, the money comes from a fund built up from any excess charges or the bill is split pro rata the flat's share of the block.

The rule of thumb is if a block has a floor space of 1,000 square metres and you flat has 100 square metres of floor space, then you pay 10% of the bill.

The problem is the freeholder may pick contractors who charge more than you feel is reasonable for the job.

You then have an option to pay up or go in to dispute with the freeholder.

Council properties

Council properties have all the problems of pointed out above relating to older and leasehold properties, plus some special issues all of their own.

Many councils are poorly maintained or of a dubious build quality that is difficult to finance.

If the building materials are not obvious, try and find out what was used – often a private neighbour with a similar house can tell you because they have financed their own purchase.

Some council properties are impossible to finance and you may have a limited number of expensive lenders available for others.

Chapter 7 - Putting A Price On Property

General condition of a property

Providing a property is structurally sound, refurbishing, like fitting a new kitchen or bathroom or changing the windows and doors is relatively cheap and easy.

Structural problems are a different matter - and these are often an issue with auction properties.

Here's some points to check out:

- Boiler age and condition

- Electric fuse boards and wiring

- Damp and condensation

- Subsidence or cracks in the wall

Does your deal stack up?

Working out if a deal stacks up for you is sitting down with pen, paper and calculator or in from of a spreadsheet to work out a few sums.

Once you have completed your due diligence you should have:

- A property valuation

- A rental assessment

- A list of expenses you need to make to take the property to the rental market

- Any red flags regarding risks that may sink the deal

Chapter 7 - Putting A Price On Property

Next, you need to calculate whether the financial outlay and risks are worth the return.

Not spending more than £5,000 to take a property to rental market is a key due diligence criteria for the Wealth Dragons. Many properties will not let in their current condition. Some need cosmetic refurbishment like painting and new carpets. Others need a lot more work.

Experience would also tell a Wealth Dragon that refurbishments always have a cost overrun, so build a contingency in to the due diligence calculation.

To an accountant, due diligence is a cost-benefits analysis. One column lists the outgoings, and the other the return on investment. As long as the return gives the required head room over the expenses, the deal works – if not, politely say no thanks and move on to the next.

Declaration

Stand up from whatever position you're in and take a deep breath. Put your hand on your heart or point your index fingers to your temples and read out loud:

1. **Due diligence is an art rather than science and I will master this art**

2. **A property's value is based on sold comparables, not sellers' asking prices**

3. **When it comes to doing due diligence, I'll need to be extremely prudent**

Now clench your fist and punch triumphantly in the air and say "I'm a Wealth Dragon"!

Chapter 8

All About No Money Down Deals

◇◇◇

In this chapter:

- *Defining a no money down deal*
- *Bridging finance explained*
- *Investing with Other People's Money*

◇◇◇

The concept is blazingly simple – how to buy property without putting your own money in to the deal.

The problem is the simplest strategies are often the most difficult to execute. No money down deals fall in to this category. The goal posts are constantly moving, and what worked fine last time is now impossible, while a strategy that was unworkable before is now a first choice tool.

The solution is a toolkit of flexible and creative strategies that give a wide range of options for financing a deal.

What is a no money down deal?

Like the advert, the deal does what it says on the tin.

You put as little of your own money in to the transaction as possible – but this does not mean you cannot leverage other people's cash.

Unless you have significant resources, if you are raising cash from your property portfolio to finance new deals, sooner or later you will hit a glass ceiling that stops you moving on. No money down deals are the solution for professional investors who want to build a big portfolio quickly to gain their financial freedom.

Leveraging other people's money lets a property investor shatter that glass ceiling so they can keep on moving onward and upwards.

Raising the cash can come from a mixture of three methods -

- Equity release by raising funds against another property from a bridging company, remortgage or further advance

- A joint venture with a cash-rich investor

- Cash input - from your own funds, relatives or some other resource

Why a valuation is key to the deal

Recording the property valuation at the initial purchase stage is a key step for latter refinancing.

If the lender agrees to a mortgage of 75% loan-to-value, that means 75% of the purchase price or valuation, whichever is lower.

If a home is valued at £100,000 but sells for £70,00 as a 30% below-market value deal, the lender takes the transaction amount as £70,000.

If that amount is recorded at the Land Registry, any plans to remortgage after six months are scuppered because a surveyor or lender just will not accept the property is worth significantly more in the current market.

To make the deal work, the Land Registry price should reflect the £100,000 valuation.

When the valuer revisits the transaction when you refinance after waiting six months, borrowing against the actual value rather than the below-market purchase value is easier to accomplish.

This valuation should also have support from other similar homes in the area that have sold for around £100,000.

How deposit bridging works

Follow this deposit bridging deal step-by-step to better understand the anatomy of the transaction:

Property valuation : £100,000 (purchase price on contract)
Mortgage lender lends: £75,000
Bridging deposit: £25,000 (Mortgage lender needs to see proof of this deposit)

On completion:

The seller's solicitor receives £100,000
(£75,000 from lender and £25,000 from bridger)
The seller keeps £70,000 (Cash on a 30% BMV deal)
The seller's solicitor pays off bridger: £30,000
Bridger returns balance after costs to buyer :£3,000

Bridging the financial gap

Also known as 100% or No Money Down, this is the main financial strategy that helps professional investors rapidly build property portfolios worth millions of pounds in double-quick time.

Bridging finance is a tool with three main applications:

Deposit bridging

The first point to make about deposit bridging is the strategy sits in a grey area and you need to make up your mind about the ethics involved.

The Wealth Dragon view is that the strategy is out there and in common use, so explaining how deposit bridging works is not advocating any investor should or should not proceed.

Nevertheless, deposit bridging is probably the most popular no money down strategy for professional investors in the UK. In deposit bridging, the mortgage is based on the full market value of the property as the purchase price.

If a property is valued at £100,000, this is the price that will go in the contract as the purchase price and the lender will make an advance based on their maximum loan-to-value criteria, like 75% or £75,000.

The seller refunds the difference between the valuation and agreed below market value purchase price as a separate arrangement unrelated to the purchase.

This is often termed the 'rebate' and is considered as the fee the seller pays the buyer for arranging the transaction.

Chapter 8 - All About No Money Down Deals

Deposit bridging needs the seller's co-operation and that's why we emphasise the importance of working directly with motivated sellers and your own legal team.

Open bridging

Open bridging means the contract has no end date. The main strategy is buying a property outright with bridging funds with the intention of refinancing with a mainstream mortgage lender.

A mainstream lender is a bank, building society or one of their subsidiaries, rather than a bridging firm. A typical scenario is buying from an auction or any other deal with a short deadline on the completion date.

Closed bridging

Close bridging is no longer available in the UK, but is common in some other countries. Banks and building societies changed their lending rules to prohibit remortgaging a property bought for cash for at least six months after purchase.

A typical close bridging scenario is buying a below market value home with an agreement to pay cash on completion in 28 days. You would immediately remortgage at completion on the higher valuation of the property.

Sometimes, property professionals call these 'back-to-back', 'instant remortgage' or 'same-day remortgage' deals.

The deal works like this:

        Property valuation: £100,000
        Below market valuation price: £70,000

Bridging finance advanced: £70,000

The seller is paid and simultaneously, the property is remortgaged:
Mortgage at 75% loan-to-value: £75,000
Bridging finance is paid: £70,000
Cash back to cover fees and costs: £5,000

Any money remaining from the cash back after settling the bills goes to the buyer.

Equity Release

Equity release or draw down is a less contentious strategy than deposit bridging – but places that glass ceiling on an investors ability to build a portfolio beyond the limit of the cash released by refinancing property already owned.

This strategy only works in a housing market fuelled by price inflation.

For example, an investor purchases a buy to let for £100,000 on a standard 25% deposit/75% mortgage basis. After a few months in a rising market, the house value might rise to £125,000.

The investor refinance the buy to let and own to raise another cash lump sum and buys another letting property. A few months later, the properties are refinanced again to buy a third buy to let and so on.

The problems with this strategy are:

- The refinancing is limited to a percentage loan-to-value of the portfolio – currently a maximum 75% LTV

How other people's money deals work

You agree to buy a home from a motivated seller at 30% below market value and opt for an other people's money deal. This is how the numbers crunch:

On purchase:

Property valuation:	£100,000
Seller accepts:	£70,000 (The lender's pur chase price
Mortgage lender advances	£52,500 (75% LTV)
Deposit needed:	£17,500 (Borrowed from your cash rich investor)

After 6 months:

You borrow £75,000 (based on the full market value of £100,000) and after paying of the mortgage of £52,500, the tax free cash back is £22,500

You pay your investor £17,500 plus interest from the cash back.

If you pay interest at 2% per month, your investor can earn £350 x 6 = £2,100.

For the investor, the return is much more than a bank would pay as interest.

After costs, you have cash back of £22,500 - £17,500 - £2,100 = £2,900 plus a property in your ownership.

- Rent cover may cap the borrowing before the maximum LTV threshold is met

- Borrowing on the investor's home is limited by income available to service the loan

Eventually one of these factors – or a combination of all three – will put a stop to expanding the portfolio.

Spending other people's money

The Other People's Money strategy is brokering a deal with a third party involved as an investor other than a mortgage lender or bridger.

In most cases, the cash-rich investor is sitting in the bridger's chair at the table by providing all the deposit funds to complete a deal. To make the investor's involvement worthwhile to you the deal has to have some benefits –

- The investor offers a better rate and costs package than a bridging firm

- You can't raise bridging finance for some reason

- If your cash-rich investor wants to pitch the finance package in or around the level of a bridging firm, then you have to work out whether the deal is worthwhile.

In other cases, the cash–rich investor may help out with extra, quick cash for covering a refurbishment.

Lease options introduced

A lease option is a contract between a home owner and an investor that gives the investor control of the property and any rental income without a change of ownership or mortgage lender.

This is an ideal solution for dealing with property owners who have little or no equity, but need to move on.

Lease option contracts are popular in the USA and Australia, where they are termed as 'rent to own' or 'lease options' or 'options to buy'.

Find out more about lease options in Chapter 9.

Declaration

Stand up from whatever position you're in and take a deep breath. Put your hand on your heart or point your index fingers to your temples and read out loud:

1. **There are different No Money Down techniques available and I will use them to build a portfolio fast**

2. **Deposit bridging is a "grey area" and I will take personal responsibility in deciding whether to use it or not**

3. **Since I am serious about investing in property, I WILL master lease options**

Now clench your fist and punch triumphantly in the air and say "I'm a Wealth Dragon"!

Chapter 9

The Lowdown On Lease Options

Lease options give property investors a flexible strategy to negotiate winning deals with motivated sellers – especially if a below market deal is not available because the homeowner has little or no equity. This chapter is a quick guide to lease options – if you want to know more, look up the book *"Step by Step Guide to Lease Options"* by the Wealth Dragons Vincent Wong and John Lee.

Who should look at lease options

Lease options are ideal for any serious investor, but they are an excellent tool for those with an indifferent credit history.

No matter where you are in the world, if you can't get a mortgage, you can still access a lease option strategy regardless of your financial past. Lease options are also the ideal tool for investors looking for cash-flow who are not bothered about the equity in the property.

What is a lease option?

Just think about it – there are two things you'll need to control in order to control the property.

- The price

- The cash flow

If you control the above, it's the same as "owning" a property with a mortgage. You may live in the property, let it out, decorate it and when the time comes for you to sell, you have the right to do so.

In a nutshell, a lease option gives you a right but no obligation to purchase a property for a pre-agreed price during a specific period of time.

In the meantime, the leaseholder takes over the property from the owner by continuing to service the mortgage with a view to buying the home.

It's important to understand the buyer has an option but not the obligation to buy the property.

Lease options – key points

Leaseholders and home owners can structure the deals any way they want but every lease option has common points:

- The owner grants an option to the leaseholder to buy the property

- Exercising the option has to take place on or before an agreed date

- The option price of a property is agreed at the start of the contract

- In the UK, rent back to the owner under a lease option is not possible

- The owner is bound by the terms of the contract, but the leaseholder can opt out at any time before the completion date

Lease option benefits for investors

Lease options present investors with an easy way to earn cash from a property without all the hassle that goes with ownership:

Reduced Risk - If a lease option deal goes wrong with the deal, you can walk away without any financial implications

No Finance - The main benefit of lease options is the fact that you can acquire a property without a mortgage in the short term.

Cash Flow - The difference between the seller's mortgage payment and the rent received is profit.

Capital Gains - Agreeing a price today due in the future means any price rise during the lease option period is a bonus

Lease option benefits for sellers

So why would a seller be willing to agree to fix a price with you today and let you take over the property?

Little or No Equity - Sellers in financial difficulty can release income tied up in mortgage repayments even if they cannot deliver a below market value deal because they have little or no equity.

Profit share – Selling now with no equity is unattractive to many homeowners, but building a profit share that guarantees a future cash lump sum is an attractive proposition

Pitching lease options to a seller

A lease option is not a one-size-fits-all strategy, the structure is elastic and the solution can stretch as a tailored solution to meet the individual needs of most owners.

Property investors sometimes make their own difficulties by labelling a deal as a lease option and then trying to sell the package to an owner.

Think of selling a car. The salesman does not lift the bonnet and explain the complexities of a V8 diesel injection engine with an overhead cam – instead the salesman concentrates on the perceived benefits of owning the vehicle.

It's good to remember that however little you know about lease options, your knowledge of the topic is far in excess of any property owner's.

What you really need to know is how to communicate with a homeowner. You can find out more about sales and negotiation skills in Chapter 10.

The first rule of lease options

Remember lease options are like Brad Pitt's Fight Club – the first rule of the lease options is not to talk about them.

How a lease option deal works

Lease options give property investors a vast number of variations on a theme to complete a deal.

Here's an example:

A homeowner has a property worth £100,000 with a mortgage of £100,000. The owner wants to sell, but is financially hamstrung because any proceeds from a sale are swallowed by redeeming the mortgage even before considering estate agent fees and other costs.

Taking an offer of less than £100,000 won't pay off the mortgage and it's doubtful the owner could raise another mortgage if he moved on. The owner talks to a property investor who suggests structuring a lease option deal.

The investor can see the rent received would cover the mortgage and any running costs while leaving a tidy cash profit each month.

Step one is agreeing a price with the owner. The investor negotiates a lease option with the owner that allows a property purchase in seven years for £100,000. This clears the debt for the owner, who does not have to pay the mortgage meanwhile, and gives the investor a below-market-value option for a no money down deal.

Step two is a sandwich option. The investor then finds a tenant who agrees to buy the home for £130,000 just before the investor's option with the owner expires.

Continued on next page >

> *< Continued from previous page*
>
> The tenant believes the property will be worth £140,000 then, so the asking price is a bargain.
>
> The investor sits smartly in the middle of the lease options – on the one side is a below market value deal and on the other, a sale to the tenant.
>
> At the end of the option, providing the house prices move as expected, the investor picks up a property worth £140,000 for £100,000 and then immediately sells the property on for £130,000.
>
> Throughout the term of the lease option, the tenant is paying the mortgage from the rent and the investor is receiving a cash flow as well.
>
> Everyone seems happy with the agreement – the owner moves on with a plan in place to clear the debt, the investor structures a profitable deal and the tenant buys a home for a good price.

Many UK homeowners find lease options a confusing concept because of their unfamiliarity with the term. So, strip out the jargon and technical explanations and work on the benefits. Look at the strategy stripped down for more clues about how to broach a lease option solution with a home owner:

Eliminate Other Options

Cash is the incentive for motivated sellers – they are talking to you because they need money fast. Not every property has the head room for a below market deal and if you are not talking cash, they will soon lose interest.

Chapter 9 - The Lowdown On Lease Options

You need to explain why a cash sale is not feasible under their financial circumstances, while pointing out that leaving the house on the market is not an option if a fast sale is required.

Once the seller runs out of options, then they are ready to hear your proposal. Leads with little or no equity that other investors throw away are potentially good candidates for a lease option.

Find out about their mortgage

Lease options are cash flow deals that are not as price sensitive as below-market-value purchases. A lease option builds time in to a deal that lets a property grow in price.

While waiting for the deal to mature, you need to let the property at a rent that will cover the costs and give you money in your pocket.

Don't forget your due diligence and find out all you can about the mortgage – the terms, the interest rate, and if the payments are in arrears. Next, check out the likely rent you can achieve.

Test close

Ask the home owner a crucial question: "If you no longer have to pay your mortgage every month or deal with any issues related to your property, would that allow you to move on with your life?"

For the owner, a lease option gives the same net effect on income as selling as the mortgage is now paid for out of someone else's pocket.

Read more about the test close in Chapter 10.

Chapter 9 - The Lowdown On Lease Options

Explain your proposal in simple terms

Focus on the benefits, forget the jargon and keep things simple.

Don't say you will take an option on the property so you can buy at some time in the future, say something like: "I'll keep paying your mortgage until I'm can buy your home. Meanwhile, you don't have to worry because I'll take care of the mortgage for you".

Examining a real life lease option deal

A simplified transcript from a recent lease option deal that Vincent Wong discussed with a home owner is included as Appendix A

Getting started as a lease options investor

It doesn't matter where you are from, lease option strategies are the same. With the credit crunch making mortgage borrowing a challenge for many investors, lease options are something every investor can promote.

As the UK's leading experts and the first authors to write a book about lease options, we offer a sell-out One-Day Lease Options Intensive Course that will teach you all you need to know.

For further details, call +44 (0)1908 698873 or visit *www. LearnLeaseOptions.co.uk.*

Declaration

Stand up from whatever position you're in and take a deep breath. Put your hand on your heart or point your index

fingers to your temples and read out loud:

1. When I have a mortgage on a property, I don't own it. The bank does!

2. Property investment is about control. I can use lease options to control properties without using a mortgage or a deposit

3. In a lease option, it is my responsibility to communicate the idea to the seller

4. I will learn everything about lease options and become an expert in it

Now clench your fist and punch triumphantly in the air and say "I'm a Wealth Dragon"!

Chapter 10

The Most Important Millionaire Skill

◇◇◇

In this chapter:

- *Understanding the art of negotiation*
- *The 10 rules of negotiation*
- *How to communicate effectively*

◇◇◇

Someone hungry for success, like a sports star, musician, lawyer or artist, invests an enormous amount of time and effort in to training.

Yet property professionals who face tough make or break decisions on most days never go beyond reading a few books or articles.

Understanding how to influence decisions lets you take control of a property deal – and switches the balance from failing to close on potential leads to becoming a successful property millionaire.

Why training is vital in property

Understanding people and what makes them tick is really important to a property investor.

Property is a people business that involves life-changing decisions.

The decisions you make affect you, your family those you buy

114

property from and their families.

Here are some of the people you will regularly meet:

Motivated sellers

The clue is in the name. A motivated seller generally has a financial reason for wanting to speak to a cash buyer offering a quick sale.

Sellers with time go to estate agents

You need to find their motivation quickly – and dispense with those who are not ready to make a deal.

Estate agents

Dealing with estate agents needs powerful communication skills that makes you stand out from the crowd. You have to give them a reason to pass you deals.

Joint venture partners

A key issue with joint venture partners who may invest time or cash with you is trust. They have to trust you with their money and trust you to do what you say when you say you will. Talking a good deal is not good enough with these guys, they expect you to close deals and make them money as well.

Tenants

Landlords never pick up a telephone call from a tenant praising them because they have provided a smart, clean home where everything works. You only hear from tenants who want something – they are looking for a property, want to complain about a property or renegotiate the rent. Tenants are customers just like sellers, so you need to keep them happy while maintaining control of the relationship.

Property professionals

Solicitors, accountants, mortgage brokers, surveyors, builders, insurers, printers – the list goes on and many of these people have special needs.

The secret of your success

A business cannot survive without sales.

In Chapter 3, effective marketing was identified as a key property investment activity.

Sales and negotiation build on that foundation. The strange fact is most entrepreneurs avoid selling because they fear the role is beneath them or they do not like rejection.

Successful sales people have no such fears and are spurred on by results. Successful negotiators are skilled communicators who can interact with people at any level, from the doorman to the company chairman.

Both topics command several volumes of their own, but here are some sales and negotiation basics to give you some food for thought:

Hitting the hot button

Everyone has a hot button so you'll need to find it as soon as possible to make that connection. One way to achieve this is to listen and find clues.

Chapter 10 - The Most Important Millionaire Skill

The clues will drop out in the conversation as you talk to someone. If you are in their home or office, try looking at pictures and books for some clue about their interests and change the topic to find some common ground.

You want them to do business, but a general rule for most people is if you don't like them, you will not do business with them.

So, you want them to like you not because the attention reinforces your ego, but because they are more likely to do close a deal with you.

Switch off that selling mode when you first meet someone and slip in to building a rapport instead.

Another way to make instant connection is by mirroring and matching. Have you ever had a telephone conversation with someone who spoke fast with lots of energy and you became frustrated and vice versa?

One tip is to match how the seller speaks in their pitch, speed, tone, rhythm etc. This automatically builds connection and rapport. In most cases, you do this subconsciously but look for times when you need to make and effort to keep in sync with another person.

Making people visualise their pain

People generally make decisions based on emotional reasons. One of these emotional reasons is pain and over 90% of us make decisions based on avoiding pain.

Take a toothache that you ignored but later became so painful you had to go to the dentist. That's the pain factor.

Chapter 10 - The Most Important Millionaire Skill

A seasoned negotiator can literally show people what pain their pain looks like.

Effective negotiators are effective communicators. You must have the ability to influence how people think and paint pictures with words.

Many homeowners are simply in denial about the reality of their financial hardships and the likely outcomes. You need to help them face their reality.

If someone is facing repossession ask questions like:

- "Do you realise what will happen once you get repossessed?"

- "How much interest a day do you pay on your mortgage arrears?"

- "Where will you live when the house is repossessed?"

- "What will happen to your family when they lose their home?"

Pain is the number one motivation factor for most people. Unless they can sense pain, they won't take action.

Effective "pain questions" elicit honest answers.

Don't make statements that could make you appear insensitive or heavy-handed, but ask them their opinions about the likely outcome of repossession.

This method makes the seller tell you the consequences of failing to agree action or how life would improve if they let you take over the mortgage payments using a lease option.

Chapter 10 - The Most Important Millionaire Skill

Watching your words

Good communicators have a self-awareness choose their words carefully and have an intrinsic understanding about their meaning.

Take someone who says: "You're a really nice person but..."

'But' is a connecting word and the listener is waiting for a qualification or explanation of the first phrase that's generally negative when someone says 'But'.

Picture driving a car you've just bought out of the showroom as the salesman says: "By the way don't worry about the clutch." What are you thinking now?

Remember language and choice of words shapes the way people think as well as how they feel.

What you say and how you say is often the difference between closing a lease option deal and leaving empty-handed.

The solution is think about what you are saying rather than what to say.

The 10 rules of negotiation

If you bear this simple points in mind when negotiating, you should close more deals:

1. Get the seller to like you

This may seem obvious but you could win a deal just on the basis that the seller likes you more than the other buyer and wants to do business with you.

Chapter 10 - The Most Important Millionaire Skill

Most sellers are unfamiliar with private home sales so they are more likely to accept a lower offer from someone they trust rather than risking their most costly asset to someone who appears dishonest.

2. Listen

You should listen 90% of the time and talk only when necessary.

If you don't listen to the seller, you'll miss a lot of the important signs and signals about the seller's needs. Once you've made a point, shut up, listen and observe the seller's reaction. Talking too much, and worse, waffling, shows you need the deal.

3. Don't show your need

No matter how much you want that deal, don't show your hand and get ready to walk away if you have to. Remember those foreign markets where the seller calls you back and settles the price just when you're about to walk away.

4. Research

Carry out thorough due diligence before discussing the nitty-gritty of a deal with a seller. Read more about due diligence in Chapter 7.

5. Don't be the first to name the figure

Don't jump in to naming a price. Listen to the seller and ask them if they have any figures.

If the seller insists that you name a price, deflect it with "what do you realistically expect from this sale?" or "it depends on the other terms so it helps if you give me your bottom-line figure".

If you must give a price, test the water with an offer that you consider ridiculously low. If it's negative, ask the seller what price they expect.

Negotiation is an art so "play it by ear"

6. Don't take "no" for an answer

When you hear "no" from the seller, respond immediately with: "Tell me more".

Find out about the seller's objections. Often they are unrelated to price.

One seller rejected an offer because a 28-day completion was "too quick" and she had booked a holiday.

Ask simple questions such as "help me understand your concerns".

7. It's OK for you not to be OK

If the seller wants to talk, it's OK. Talking is good and is building a relationship. Let the seller think he or she runs the show even though deep down you know you're the one in control. Whoever talks too much is the one who is showing needs and insecurity.

8. Use scarcity

Make an offer rare and difficult to come by so the seller appreciates your worth. Don't leave the offer open indefinitely, explain that you don't know how long another will take to find – if you can find one at all.

Create competition and tell the seller that there are lots of sellers out there who would snap up this offer, so your investor would like an answer as soon as possible.

9. Use third party authority

This is car salesmen's favourite – "I'll need to speak to my manager."

When you're bargaining, a third person, real or imagined, who's supposedly the decision maker takes responsibility away from you and makes haggling difficult for the seller.

10. Don't rush to close a deal

A deal is always subject to contract. People and circumstances can change and a deal that was not on yesterday can be alive today or vice versa. This is remorse that sometimes surfaces when a seller bases a decision on emotion. Before closing, try and make sure that a seller's decision is informed and based on considering all the circumstances, not just emotion.

Negotiation step-by-step

Scripts are rigid and do not give buyers room to manoeuvre – so here's a breakdown of how to talk to a motivated seller:

Introduction

Tell them who you are and why you are calling – filling an online form is the seller inviting you to call, so tell them who you are and that you are phoning because they asked.

An opening could go like this: "Hi, it's John calling from Network Property Buyers. You filled in an enquiry form from our web site this morning about selling your property so I'm just calling you to see how we can help."

Open questions

The person who talks least controls the conversation. Listen. Encourage the seller to speak with open questions that require detailed answers.

They are excellent tools because they let you break barriers. Try questions like: "Tell me a bit about your situation to see how we may help you?" or "So what got you selling your property?"

If you start a conversation by asking specific or close questions, you could end up getting short answers.

Throw in hooks

Sometimes you might have to throw in more than one hook to get your attention so you'll need to listen to the person's response.

A strong hook when opening a conversation might be: "The reason for calling is that we have a buyer who is ready to give you a cash offer for your property but just to need to ask you a few more questions first".

Ask for permission

Some sellers could get offended if you asked them personal questions or questions they perceived as relevant to the sale. For example, you need to know the outstanding mortgage balance to settle on a strategy. The strategy depends on the enquiry in the property. A good question to ask is: "So I can offer you the best solution for your situation, I'll be asking you some questions regarding your property and your finances, would that be OK?"

Say it matter-of-factly and don't make a big deal out of it.

Uncover

However good your due diligence, you won't know the seller's motivation for sure until you speak to them. Three key factors can help you decide how ready they are to sell. We call this the Wealth Dragon Motivation triangle and the three sides are:

> *Motivation* - Since you're a cash buyer and you only deal with motivated sellers, you'll need to find out about the seller's motivation.
>
> *Time* - Another way of identifying how motivated the seller is to find out how quickly they need to sell.
>
> *Equity* - The level of equity has direct relevance to the strategy you can use to help the seller. If the seller has little or no equity in the property, then go for lease options. Otherwise, you would need 25 – 30% BMV for a no money down deal.

As soon as you find out how much equity is in the property, you can pitch your solution.

Eliminate options

People sometimes don't understand their options until you show them.

For example, if someone is desperate to sell within a month and they insist on leaving the property with an estate agent, then it's not really an option, even if the seller seems to think so.

It's to you as a consultant to eliminate impracticable considerations to leave the real options.

Test closing

Test closing is not the same as closing but more of a general mood assessment. People generally don't commit straight away.

Test closing is letting the seller make small, incremental commitments until you sense they are ready to close.

Here are a couple of typical test-closing questions: "If I could complete on the sale within 28 days, would you go ahead with it?"or "If I could take care of your mortgage, would that mean you could move on with your life quickly without further financial worries?"

A real sale word-by-word

Read a word-by-word transcript of a real sales negotiation in Appendix B.

Declaration

Stand up from whatever position you're in and take a deep breath. Put your hand on your heart or point your index fingers to your temples and read out loud:

1. I have the power to change myself regardless of

Chapter 10 - The Most Important Millionaire Skill

my upbringing and conditioning

2. I love sales because I am successful. I love being sold to and embrace every opportunity to sell to others

3. When I negotiate, I will use the three communication builders and ten rules of negotiation

4. If I want to get someone's attention, I'll throw in a strong "hook"

Now clench your fist and punch triumphantly in the air and say "I'm a Wealth Dragon"!

Handling Leads and Packaged Deals

<><><><><><><><><><><><><><><><><><><><><><><><><><><><><><><><>

In this chapter:

- *Understanding the importance of leads*
- *Packaged deals explained*
- *12 steps to a property completion*

<><><><><><><><><><><><><><><><><><><><><><><><><><><><><><><><>

It's really important that you don't get mixed up between a packaged deal or a ready-made deal and property leads. Leads are not negotiated deals.

A lead is just information disclosed by motivated sellers who have expressed an interest to talk to cash investors. But by no means have they agreed upon or signed anything.

A typical lead will probably sell from between £25 to £125, depending on how motivated a seller is, how much information there is in a lead, the location of the property, cash-flow and the price.

Defining and qualifying leads

Successfully converting a lead involves tapping into the mind of the seller to identify his / her needs which cannot be done online.

If you already know the seller is very motivated, i.e. already agreed to consider a 25% BMV offer during the enquiry, it is your goal to convert it into a deal that is 25%, 30% or above

Chapter 11 - Handling Packaged Leads and Deals

using your negotiation skills. Lead qualification is about asking the right questions to establish the level of motivation of the seller and not negotiating on behalf of the buyer.

The negotiation only begins the moment the buyer engages with the seller.

Whether you are buying leads from a lead seller or generating your own leads, this is a golden rule to remember: "The more questions you ask sellers during the enquiry, the less likely these sellers would give you the answers and the higher the cost of generating your leads."

Even the so called "telephone contacted" leads as a basis of qualification simply confirm the contact details of the seller. They do NOT establish the basic motivation level any better than a good online qualifying process.

Therefore, it is important to recognise that a telephoned contacted lead does not equate to a qualified lead if inappropriate and insufficient questions have been asked.

Many sellers do agree to a 25% preliminary offer online but the extra 5% will require the extra effort from the part of the buyer.

After all, it is easier to move from an expected 25% BMV to 30% than from 0% to 30% BMV.

Don't forget simply by correcting the seller's own estimated value of the property using your own research as evidence could easily gain you that extra few percentage BMV you require.

After all, in today's market, establishing a property's market value is subjective and more of an art than science.

Chapter 11 - Handling Packaged Leads and Deals

How do I convert leads?

With pre-negotiated property deals, there is a huge jump in the price. That's why negotiation skills are so important. Just because someone has agreed on a deal at a large discount, i.e. 25-30%, they can actually command a fee of £5,000 or £10,000 upwards.

By mastering your negotiation skills, you can turn a lead into a deal and save yourself thousands. Basically, what you lack in skill you make up for in numbers.

So if you have no idea how to negotiate and are new, you just simply call up one hundred people and the odds would say you are bound to get a person who's willing to give you a good discount, up to 30% or more.

However if you are more experienced and have good negotiation skills, you can actually get these numbers to work much more in your favour. A good negotiator, like John, can actually get a conversion of one in seven. In other words, we get one deal for every seven leads that come to us.

What are packaged deals?

A packaged deal is a deal where the lead has already been sourced (i.e. someone has already done the leg work to find this deal directly from a motivated seller), negotiations have taken place, and the whole process is actually managed by the deal provider. A packaged deal is something that comes in a package.

How do you find a packaged deal?

To obtain a packaged deal you need to be able to get a mortgage so check that your credit record is clean and you have not been late on payments.

The three credit agencies are Experian, Equifax and Call Credit. You also need to make sure you have advance funds (which vary according to the packager you use) For example survey, mortgage broker fees, advance reservation fees of around 1% to secure the deal.

Why do packaged deals?

Packaged deals are useful if you are time-poor, have some money to invest and you don't want to actually source the below market value property leads yourself.

Perhaps you don't necessarily have the negotiation skills to influence sellers to offer you properties at substantially below the market value or even the time to manage the whole deal process?

Negotiating and agreeing on a deal is probably one of the easiest parts of the deal process. Getting from negotiation to completion involves a lot of work.

In any property deal, you have to have a very good team at hand. For example solicitors, a mortgage broker, a bridging loan financier, perhaps builders. All these things are managed by a packaged deal provider.

If you have some spare cash and you don't have the time to source your leads or deal with solicitors and mortgage brokers, buy a packaged deal.

Especially in a rising market, whatever fee you pay up-front on a packaged deal will be offset against the property price.

Chapter 11 - Handling Packaged Leads and Deals

How do you find leads?

If you're an investor, you should start making an effort to attend networking events. You will find people who can offer you leads and deals. You can leave your name and phone number with them and be put on their database and they will send you an email when the deal comes along. In the email it will outline the details of this deal with the level of discount and the property particulars.

How to make thousands a month from being a deal packager? Now that you've learnt all about communication and negotiation from John from the previous chapter, you're in a much better position than other investors because you have the skills to do deals.

There are lots of amateur or arm-chaired investors who don't mind paying some money for each deal so it is your chance to make some income while you're building your portfolio. You never know – you might even be able to give up your job. There are many packaged deal providers out there who do this full time.

How to start packaging

If you're generating your own leads and some of them don't fall within your buying criteria, it doesn't mean someone else wouldn't want those deals. So why not close them and make some money?

Leads

There's a saying in the business that "the person who has the leads is the daddy" because this daddy can play the numbers game and make lots of money from flipping deals.

A lock-out agreement

When you agree a deal with a seller, you'll need to have exclusivity for this deal and make sure the seller doesn't sell the property to someone else for a period of time. Otherwise, your investor could lose money from day one for valuation and solicitor's fees.

The best way to secure a deal is to use a Purchase Option Agreement. This gives you the right but not the obligation to buy the property exclusively from a seller at a pre-determined period, usually 3 months.

If you would like a free copy of the Purchase Option Agreement, visit *www.NetworkPropertyInvestment.co.uk* and follow the link Free Option Agreement Download.

Building a list

Once you get your deal negotiated, you need to off-load this deal to your investor colleagues.

That's why networking is important. You need to have a list of investors on your books. The question you need to ask is, "How many people do you know that know you are in the property business?" If there are less than five or 10, now is the time to start building your list and this is easy.

Basically, every person you come across, just exchange business cards and tell them that you're looking for property deals or that you've got great property deals you are ready to pass onto other people for a fee.

Lots of people who are not already in the property business are willing to pay a small fee to get no money down deal. The bigger your list, the more chance you have to off-load a deal.

Chapter 11 - Handling Packaged Leads and Deals

Like lead conversion, it's very much a numbers game. An excellent place to start is to attend one of your local Wealth Dragons Unleashed events. To register for an event near you, visit: *www.WealthDragonsUnleashed.co.uk.*

Marketing

There are a number of ways in which you can make numbers stack better for you. One way is to make your packaged deals very attractive to investors.

Selling anything is a marketing exercise, so you need to know the fundamentals of marketing. If you've got a deal with a good discount, how are you going to put it together in a sales letter or an email to show an investor that it's a great deal?

One way of doing it is with pictures -there is a saying that, 'A picture paints a thousand words'.

Ask the seller if they can send you some pictures of the property or when you are with the seller ask their permission to go round and take some.

If you have some photographs in your marketing material, the investor will have a strong idea of the condition of the property. Also give a good description of the property.

Make a special note of features such as double glazed, central heating/boiler, garden, sizes of rooms, construction etc. It's no different from any other marketing exercise.

Another way to make a deal attractive is to sell the deal's profitability to the investor. For example:

- Investor puts in £5,000 to buy the deal and makes an instant equity of £30,000 on completion.

- Investor puts in £5,000 to make £250 of net cash flow each month. This is equivalent to 60% return on investment per annum

Supply and demand

If you have a deal in an area where there is huge demand, for example in New York City or London, then you'll probably find that the deal will go very quickly. Some people will be happy to give you a higher packaged deal fee for this deal. Again, different investors have got different investment criteria, so if you've got a bigger list, you've got more chance of selling a deal.

Working out what to charge

The most important thing for doing packaged deals is the fee.

Pricing is very important because marketing is about packaging, pricing and positioning. If you find that you're pricing a deal too high, you're going to have less demand than supply and therefore will need to adjust the pricing accordingly.

The crucial thing is to make sure that you get paid, typically when the deal completes. You'll probably take a deposit upfront to make sure that whoever is buying the packaged deal is serious. You can actually refund the deposit on completion if you like, but if someone is not willing to part with any cash, the likelihood is that this person is not really serious.

Make sure that whoever buys your deal has got the cash, finances in place or is eligible for a mortgage if applicable. You need to do what we call a 'decision in principle' in the UK.

You put the investor in touch with a mortgage broker, who will run the investor's details through the system and come back quickly to say whether the investor is eligible for a mortgage or not.

Again, the fee you can command is subject to supply and demand and you may need to adjust it depending on the feedback.

Your team

When working on packaged deals, you must make sure that your team is solid. Your team consists of your solicitors, mortgage broker and – if the property is to be refurbished – builders.

Every step of the process needs to be managed because it is in your interest for the deal to go through quickly and efficiently. The sooner and smoother it goes through, the sooner you'll get paid. Trust us, you can get paid a lot of money just by doing packaged deals.

One word of warning though – chasing different parties for updates could be a frustrating experience, especially if you have a seller who is very anxious to complete quickly. Therefore, choosing you team is important and you'll need to be organised

The 12-step completion process

Here is the entire process for selling a packaged deal;

1. Agree the price with the seller

2. Ask the seller to sign a lock-out agreement

3. Request photographs from the seller

4. Structure the deal and highlight the best features

5. Send the deal profile to your database

6. Make your deals "first come first served" and take a deposit from the first investor

7. Put your investor in touch with a mortgage broker to get a mortgage "decision in principle". If the investor fails, move on to the next one on the list

8. Instruct a valuation for the investor through the mortgage broker

9. If valuation comes back OK, instruct the solicitors. If not, consider an appeal or re-negotiate with the seller

10. Once the mortgage offer has been issued, arrange for bridging if required

11. Set a date for exchange of contracts

12. Complete

There are so many different ways in which you can package a deal and make money from it. We run a very popular workshop in our office in Milton Keynes. For those of you outside the UK, if you want to know more about packaged deals and learn how to package a deal in your country, call +44 (0)1908 698873.

Declaration

Stand up from whatever position you're in and take a deep breath. Put your hand on your heart or point your index

fingers to your temples and read out loud:

1. A lead is not a deal but I can use my sales and negotiation skills to convert them

2. I can make lots of money by negotiating and flipping deals to others

3. The more leads I have, the more money I can make

Now clench your fist and punch triumphantly in the air and say "I'm a Wealth Dragon"!

Systemising Your Property Business

◇◇

In this chapter:

- *Working smart by systemising*
- *Shifting responsibilities on to others*
- *The importance of the Pareto Principle*

◇◇

The difference between working for a business and working for yourself is a business runs when you are not there.

Many self-employed make a lifestyle choice to work for themselves, but they don't so much run a business as have a self-employed job.

Successful business people do not have to give up their lives in return for the rewards they reap. Working smart by systemising your property investments will win back time and make you more efficient.

The importance of systemisation

From day one of your property business, aim to build a pipeline or workflow that takes in leads at one end and pushes out completed purchases at the other end.

Starting a business, it's easy to fall in to the micro management trap and the danger of self employment. The danger signs are:

- Unable to take holidays or time off

- Long and unpredictable hours

- Working on controlling rather than expanding the business

- Taking work problems home

- Limited social life

- The only person you can depend on is yourself

Shifting responsibility

Stepping across the road from self employment to running a business needs a change of mindset for the entrepreneur. You have to hand responsibility over to others and trust them to do their jobs. Saving money is cited as the main reason for failing to delegate, but it's not necessarily true.

Property is a fast moving business. You need to be ahead of the game and respond quickly to the market and manage your properties effectively otherwise you will miss out.

As a business owner you should delegate everything that can be done by someone else. The systemised investor has professional tradesman lined up to renovate a property straight after completion. Time is money; the sooner the property is renovated, the sooner viewings can start and the sooner a tenant can move in.

The Pareto Principle

Pareto was an Italian economist born in 1848, who observed that 20% of something is often responsible for 80% of the result.

Chapter 12 - Systemising Your Property Business

For example, in business, 20% of customers are probably responsible for 80% of the sales. This is known as the 80-20 rule or Pareto Principle.

You'll probably find that 20% of the daily activities are responsible for 80% of the results generated. You can apply the 80-20 rule to almost anything.

The principle translates in to systemising your business, what you're looking for is the 20% of your efforts that will deliver 80% of the result.

For example, if you're sourcing property deals, you want to look at channels where 20% of your advertising budget will give you 80% of the actual result.

What you might need to do is compare your online advertising campaign against leaflets or newspaper ads, to find out where the 80% of results come from.

Systemisation for your property portfolio

Sooner or later the time and hassle involved in managing properties starts to slow down your investment activities.

Many property investors start out by managing their own portfolio, which is fine if you have three or four properties in a single location.

The trouble is, as a portfolio grows, the administration expands as well and many property investors find they are bogged down with calls from tenants, keeping the books and managing tradesmen.

The answer is to systemise your business and employ a property manager. Your manager can handle all the administration

– including the pipeline progress of buying new properties.

The manual should cover every aspect of your business from advertising, looking after property maintenance, collecting rent and finding tenants to keeping the books.

A single manager paid a salary or an hourly rate is cheaper and more effective than several expensive letting agents in different towns and cities.

A property manager fees time for the investor by removing the day-to-day management of the business. Although the salary costs money, the overall savings more than compensate for the outlay.

Benefits of systemisation

Systemising a business saves money and lets the business trade more efficiently.

Take this book. In a way you are benefitting from the Wealth Dragons systemising their knowledge of the property business. You can take advantage of years of knowledge at your own pace and keep the book as a reference.

What you need to do is look at your business to identify opportunities for systemising.

Declaration

Stand up from whatever position you're in and take a deep breath. Put your hand on your heart or point your index fingers to your temples and read out loud:

1. In order to have a successful business, I'll need to

systemise it so I may focus my efforts on what creates value

2. I will apply the 20:80 rule in everything I do

3. I own a business and am not a slave to my business!

Now clench your fist and punch triumphantly in the air and say "I'm a Wealth Dragon"!

Chapter 13

Making Money From Your Property Skills

◇◇

In this chapter:
- *How the Pillar System works*
- *Applying the Pillar System to your business*
- *Different ways of making money from property*

◇◇

Buying, selling and letting are not the only ways to make money from property.

As an astute investor, you have skills and experience that are a commodity other investors can buy to develop their own businesses.

Selling your services to these investors creates other valuable income streams.

The Wealth Dragons have invested a lot of time and money learning how to do this through the Pillar System.

The Pillar System

The Pillar System, that derives from the work of marketing guru Jay Abraham (*www.abraham.com*), relates to exploiting many different channels to bring sales to your business.

Imagine your business as a diving board supported by one leg. If leg goes, your business will fall. What is more ideal is a pillar system, a Greek Parthenon, with many supporting pillars each representing an income stream.

Chapter 13 - Making Money From Your Property Skills

If one pillar is removed, your business will remain standing.

The more pillars you have, the more ways you have of making money.

The car industry was a one pillar business for many suppliers to factories like Rover. The car maker tied the suppliers in to exclusive contracts, which was fine when the going was good, but when the UK car industry collapsed, the suppliers went as well.

The property industry has a similar example – the demise of the lender Mortgage Express.

Many investors relied on Mortgage Express for financing below market value properties as the lender allowed remortgage after just one day of owning the property.

This helped investors withdraw equity and reinvest their capital in more properties.

Mortgage Express was one of the first casualties of the credit crunch, and when this source of funding disappeared, many investors pulled out the market. They only had one method of property investing and didn't know how to make money any other way.

Applying the Pillar System

The crux of the pillar system is by following the way of the Wealth Dragons, by looking at your skills, you can also create different income strategies.

For example, the Wealth Dragons run a business called Deal Closer. Deal Closer helps other investors make money. Property investors can commission Deal Closer to negotiate and close deals for them.

Deal Closer charges £135 upfront and a 2% fee based on the property's valuation on completion for picking up the phone up and speaking to a seller.

Our thinking is if we can make someone £10,000 by lending them our time and skills, they can afford to pay us a reasonable fee for our efforts.

Wealth Dragons can charge for advice because they can pick up a phone and buy a house within 24 hours and that house will make someone £300 - £400 a month in positive cash flow.

Different sources of property income

The Wealth Dragons have a broad-based property business that generates income from several pillars.

Here are some of the things that we do – and it's by no means an exhaustive list.

It's up to you what you want to do, but make sure you charge others for leaning on your skills, time and knowledge.

After all, you make an investment and devoted your time in learning from our mentoring programme so it's only fair that people pay you to benefit from your knowledge.

Leafleting

One investor saw an opportunity for free marketing with leaflet campaigns. As he delivers leaflets for other businesses, he posts his own property brochures through the letter box.

Chapter 13 - Making Money From Your Property Skills

Web sites

If you're good at lead generation and have internet skills, you can help others with their online marketing.

One of our students charges other investors £1,000 to design a web site. The Wealth Dragons offer a similar service. We help people compete against us and time and time again those we have helped work with us as joint venture partners.

Managing lettings

When a portfolio grows to 10 or 20 properties, you will probably need to hire someone to look after them for you. If you have 20 houses and you're paying a 10% management fee, why not start up your own lettings company and do that for other people?

If you're going to rent property in, say Milton Keynes or Manchester, then just find other people who want their properties let and charge them 10% for doing it.

Packaged deals

Packaged deals are a way to make money from deals you don't want. If you've got lots of leads that you don't want or can't handle you can also sell these on instead of throwing them away.

Joint ventures

Here's a tip on investing in property risk-free. You find property for a partner and charge them a premium for the service. The agreement is you find the property and charge 50% of the rent but the partner is responsible for the purchase, finding tenants and the maintenance. You should also take a 50% cut of any sale price.

Consulting and mentoring

As an established property professional with an air of success, people will ask you for advice. The Wealth Dragons charge £400 an hour or £5,000 for the day for this service. The cost is reasonable because our clients can learn in a day what has taken us years to find out.

Property viewings

Several services are involved here –

- Marketing a property with photographs and video

- Escorting viewers

- Meeting surveyors

Dealing with surveyors is a popular service as having someone at a house to show the valuer around reduces the risk of the owner disclosing the purchase price and undermining the deal.

Partnership opportunities

At Wealth Dragons, we have various partnership opportunities to make money. If you want to know more, call us on +44 (0)1908 698873.

Declaration

Stand up from whatever position you're in and take a deep

breath. Put your hand on your heart or point your index fingers to your temples and read out loud:

1. I create multiple income streams

2. I will apply the Pillar System to my wealth creation

3. I'm not afraid to charge people for my skills and knowledge for which I've invested money and time

Now clench your fist and punch triumphantly in the air and say "I'm a Wealth Dragon"!

Epilogue

By Vincent Wong

The Journey Begins

Well done. You have reached a milestone with your education in the Property Millionaire Programme.

This is not the end of the journey. In fact, this is just the start. However, for reaching this far, here is some bonus material to thank you for making the commitment and being consistent with your learning.

I want to focus on three factors that I believe are critical in making a success of property and other areas of your life.

They have worked for me. I practise every day and I believe that if you follow the same action, you will produce results.

Focus

The first thing I want to share with you, which probably sounds obvious but is absolutely important is to focus on your goals and take action.

It doesn't matter what knowledge you've accumulated - if you don't get up and take action and do something, nothing will happen.

Everything has cause and effect, action and consequences. So if you've studied physics, you'll know that force = mass x acceleration.

You need to have the force to push this particular mass to move forward. You can apply this to your knowledge or any goals that you have. In order to reach those goals, you need to take action now.

Some people have a lot of excuses for inaction. Common excuses are:

- I'm too busy

- I'll do it tomorrow

- I don't understand it so I will wait

- I'm too tired

- My favourite program is on television so I'll do it some other time

If you think about it, these are nothing more than excuses. If you've got time to watch television, you have time to take action and do something about your property business.

If you've got time to go out with your friends, you've got time to start some networking and do something useful. If you have the knowledge but you don't take action, in my opinion that's the same as not having the knowledge to start with.

That's how important it is. So take action now, whether you think you're on the right course or not. Just do something because once you start, you will learn through the process of doing.

Fear

As we grew up through childhood, we were pretty much controlled by this demon called fear. The thing about fear is that it's

Epilogue

not instilled in you by other people, it is in fact from within.

Through understanding and knowledge you can eliminate fear.

In fact, most of your fear never materialises. Yet fear is debilitating. It stops you from doing things. It stops you from making progress. It stops you from expanding.

We go to work and fear losing our jobs, we fear upsetting other people, we fear what other people think of us. If you have to start living a life through the eyes of other people, your life is going to be really miserable. So don't fear anything. If you have made a goal to become successful in property, don't let fear stop you.

Don't let other people tell you that it can't be done or what will happen if you fail. Most people think about what happens if they fail, but they rarely think about what happens if they don't take action and don't succeed.

The consequences would be that you would live a life without proper resources for a happy retirement. The risk of doing nothing because of fear far outweighs the possible failure you might experience.

You need to be fearless in investing either in property, in your knowledge or in marketing for your business. A lot of people are very protective and scared of parting with their money.

But remember, if you've made a lot of money, it's not really even yours.

We only have temporary custody of money. You never own those bank notes – they're just a token of exchange. Money is all about flow – we talk about the flow of cash and wealth.

Epilogue

Don't be afraid to invest, to spend money because with this flow of energy, for every pound you spend, you probably get £2 or £3 back.

If you speak to some really successful people who donate money to charity, they will tell you that the more they give out, the more they get back, either in money or in happiness, satisfaction or some sort of reward.

Failure

Failure is another ingredient that you should really embrace with open arms. It makes you stronger and you learn from any mistakes and are more likely to succeed.

All successful people have experienced some sort of failure sometime in their life.

Failure is something that you should expect. When most people experience failure, they will just give up, stop, roll over and die. But there is a choice.

One story especially sticks in my mind – during the gold rush in California, there was one particular investor who invested his entire savings and the savings of his investors on machinery to drill for gold.

After trying it for some time, he decided that he had made a mistake and gave up. He sold all his machinery to a guy who returned to the original place the guy was drilling and he found that the other guy had been only three feet away from the gold when he gave up.

In other words, if the first person had continued drilling, continued with his mission and not given up, he would have got

Epilogue

the gold. That's an important lesson. Try to apply that to some of things you've experienced in your life.

Had you not given up, would you have succeeded? So don't give up, whatever you do - life is not about how hard you hit, it's about how hard you can get hit and still move forward. It's about how much you can take and that's the ingredient of success

The world is about giving and taking and it goes round in circles. What goes around, comes around. So don't be afraid to part with your money and help other people.

The more you help people, the more you'll get back from it.

Now clench your fist and punch triumphantly in the air and say "I'm a Wealth Dragon"!

Appendix A

Examining a real lease option deal

Here's a simplified transcript from a recent lease option deal that Vincent Wong discussed with a home owner. Susan owns a 3-bedroom semi in Milton Keynes. She has little equity and needs to move because she has lost her job and cannot afford the mortgage. Susan contacted Wealth Dragons via our web site.

VINCENT: Hi, my name is Vincent and I'm calling from Network Property Buyers.

SUSAN: OK

VINCENT: The reason for my call is that you filled in an enquiry form this morning via our web site about selling your property and so I want to see how I may help you.

SUSAN: I want to see what you would offer me for my property for a quick sale.

VINCENT: No problem. I'd be glad to help. Before I go any further, I'd like to tell you that I'll ask some questions about your situation including your finances to see how best I can help you. Is that OK?

SUSAN: Yes, no problem.

VINCENT: Also, this call will be recorded for training purposes. Is that all right?

SUSAN: Yeah, that's fine.

VINCENT: OK Susan, please tell me about your situation.

Appendix A - Examining A Real Lease Option Deal

SUSAN: Well, I've recently lost my job and I really need to sell this house because I can't afford the mortgage anymore. I came across your company's web site and noticed that you're cash buyers specialising in quick sales, is that right?

VINCENT: Yes, that's correct. So, how much do you think your property is worth?

SUSAN: It's been on the market for £120,000 for the past six weeks and I haven't had any viewings at all.

VINCENT: That I can understand. The way the market is at the moment, lots of properties are on the market unsold and we've come across some properties on the market for 12 months or more.

SUSAN: I see.

VINCENT: What's the outstanding mortgage on this property?

SUSAN: Well, we remortgaged on this property 18 months ago and so the mortgage outstanding is £110,000.

VINCENT: Is there any secured loan on the property?

SUSAN: No

VINCENT: OK, here's the situation. You need to move on quickly because the mortgage every month is a burden since you've lost your job. But you've noticed that estate agents would not be the right solution for you because there's no way you can reduce the price for a quick sale.

When the agent put your property on the market for £120,000, they would have inflated the price somewhat so that you can have room for negotiation. So your property could be worth a

Appendix A - Examining A Real Lease Option Deal

lot less than that. With your outstanding mortgage of £110,000, you have little room to manoeuvre and could end up waiting months to sell.

Even if you manage to sell, in the end you would have dropped the price a few times and still have to pay the legal fees and the estate agent's commission.

SUSAN: Yes, I sort of realised that and that's why I contacted you to see if there's anything you could do to help. The property is in a good location and would be ideal for an investor. I reckon in a good market, it could be worth £140,000 or £150,000.

VINCENT: I totally appreciate what you're saying Susan. The thing is cash buyers always base their investment decisions on the property's valuation today rather than what they could be worth in the future and all honest cash investors are looking for at least 25% below the property's market value.

The reason for that is that in today's property market, investors can only raise a certain percentage of the value of the property in cash.

Contrary to what a lot of people believe, cash buyers rarely use their own cash to invest and also, investors view property investment as quite high risk in the current climate.

Therefore, they can only offer you what they can raise and based on the valuation of your property of £120,000, the most they can offer you is around £82,000 and that's if your property can be valued at £120,000.

SUSAN: I see, and £82,000 won't even cover my mortgage...

VINCENT: Yes, that's correct unfortunately. So cash buyers are not really an option for you.

Appendix A - Examining A Real Lease Option Deal

SUSAN: OK, in that case, I'll just have to leave it on the market then to see what happens.

VINCENT: Well, I might still be able to help. How much are you paying for your mortgage at the moment?

SUSAN: Around £650 a month.

VINCENT: Is that a repayment or interest only?

SUSAN: That's interest only.

VINCENT: Wow, that's quite high for interest only. Now, what if an investor could take over your mortgage payment for you so instead of each month the money comes out of your account, it will come out of the investor's account and you wouldn't have to worry about the property's maintenance. Would that be something that might benefit you?

SUSAN: Sorry you mean you would pay my mortgage for me? Oh yes it would.

VINCENT: Do you know what the rental for your property is?

SUSAN: It'll fetch about £850 I think.

VINCENT: So if I could find an investor to do that for you so you can stop paying your mortgage immediately, would you want to go for it?

SUSAN: Yes, definitely, but that sounds too good to be true.

VINCENT: I understand why you think that. We make our profit when the property increases in value in the future. That will compensate us from the risk of taking over your property your property today. Is that OK?

Appendix A - Examining A Real Lease Option Deal

SUSAN: Yes, that's fine.

VINCENT: Also, if the market does rise quicker than we expect, we might be able to offer you a share of the profit as well because that's something we do. At the moment I can't promise anything but it's definitely a possibility. Is that OK?

SUSAN: Yeah that sounds great. What's the next step?

Anyway, the conversation continued from there and the deal completed about four weeks later.

Appendix B

A real sale word-by-word

Here's a transcript of a real sales call with notes to point out communication and negotiation comments:

SELLER: Hello. Is that John?

JOHN: Yeah, how are you doing? Are you all right? You're hard to get hold of.

SELLER: Not really. I've just got a temperamental phone
JOHN: Ah, well I'm calling you back from the office so the calls are recorded for training purposes. Is that okay?

SELLER: Yep, fine.

JOHN: Can I ask you a few questions to see if we can help or not? (Permission)

SELLER: Yep.

JOHN: Perfect. Could you tell me a little about your situation and what's got you selling your property? (Open question)

SELLER: I'm a single parent with just one child still at home – he's seventeen. And I was in a relationship and it's a big house, I can't look after it, I can't afford the mortgage anymore and I just need to get rid of it.

JOHN: OK. And have you contacted any other companies in regard to selling your property?

SELLER: No, not yet.

JOHN: When would you like to sell by? (Time question)

Appendix B - A Real Sale Word-By-Word

SELLER: Three months.

JOHN: Three months, okay. Just after Christmas then, yeah?

SELLER: Yeah, yeah.

JOHN: What is your property's worth? (Equity question)

SELLER: Well, I was toying with selling it about eighteen months ago and it was valued at £160,000 with £145,000 for a quick sale, but I know that the market's changed and I just want to get rid of it really.

I can't look after it, I can't pay for it, it's too big for me and I've just really had enough. I just want to go really. So anything reasonable really.

JOHN: Yeah. What's the outstanding mortgage on the property at the moment? (Equity question)

SELLER: About £65,000 or £66,000.

JOHN: And what's that costing you a month?

SELLER: Well it's two mortgages.

JOHN: Okay.

SELLER: It was a first mortgage, and that's about £400, and the second one is something like £200. I can't pay that now.

JOHN: That's like £600, isn't it?

SELLER: Yeah, and I just want somewhere smaller and just want to rent now, you know? I'm waiting for my last son to leave home, so I just don't want it, don't need it, can't afford it,

Appendix B - A Real Sale Word-By-Word

can't do with the hassle. Because I can't pay the mortgage, so it'll be taken off me if I don't get rid of it anyway eventually. I mean, I'm not in arrears yet, but I will be. (Seller's Motivation)

JOHN: Okay. Do you understand how companies like cash buyers work? (Positioning myself as consultant)

SELLER: You offer a reduced value price for a quick sale.
JOHN: And you understand that?

SELLER: Yeah.

JOHN: Because we always say to people, if you don't really have to sell it, then try it on the open market. Is there any reason why you haven't tried the open market? (I was acting as an impartial consultant rather than just someone looking for the best price).

SELLER: I just don't want to know. I've really had enough, you know? I haven't been very well and I just can't cope with people coming round and the hassle.

And I know a lot of people say, "You're cutting off your nose to spite your face," but sometimes in your life you just have to do what's right for you. And as long as I've got a bit of money, that's all I'm bothered about, you know? I know that I'm going to be selling it for less than I probably could, but there's also the timescale and the hassle and the stress.

And I don't want any of that. I haven't got the time anyway, because I can't pay the mortgage. So I do understand all of that.

JOHN: So I guess for yourself, you know you're getting less for it than you could, but you've got a time frame. But what this'll also allow you to do is to move into somewhere smaller, quickly, give you a bit of money so you can perhaps enjoy it as well.

Appendix B - A Real Sale Word-By-Word

SELLER: That's it, a little bit of a nest egg, yeah.

JOHN: What I'll need to do is just go and speak to a few investors. (Third party authority) Just to give you an example, most investors will offer you 70% of what the house is worth, so what they would have to do is just go away and make sure the property is worth what you're saying it's worth, otherwise the offer will be reflected.

What it'll mean here is, if you've got a mortgage of say £65,000, they'll probably give you about £101,000 for it, which means you would be left with about £36,000.

SELLER: Yep, that's fine.

JOHN: Would you be happy with that? (Test closing)

SELLER: I would, I would.

JOHN: Fantastic.

SELLER: Just to get it done and dusted, no more worry and stress. Yep.

JOHN: What that allows you to do, if you rent somewhere smaller as well is that instead of your mortgage being £600, you could probably rent somewhere for about £450, couldn't you?

SELLER: Yeah, absolutely. I've looked into it, had a look around and that's what I'm thinking. And no hassle of maintaining it. Because I can't maintain this house any more. I mean, I can't afford to and I can't do the things I used to be able to do myself either.

JOHN: Right. What sort of stuff that you used to do?

Appendix B - A Real Sale Word-By-Word

SELLER: I want to be able to just phone somebody up and say, "Something's gone wrong, please help."

JOHN: What condition is the property in, by the way? Is it in good condition or...? (Now it's time to talk about the property)

SELLER: It needs a bit of TLC. For myself, it's absolutely fine, but there are bits and pieces that need doing, things that could do with changing, jigging around. It's just had a new en-suite bathroom which has recently been done but I haven't done loads for a while. It's a sound property and it's a lovely big house, a brilliant family house with loads of potential.

JOHN: Okay. So it was valued about eighteen months ago at about £160,000 and then got reduced to £145,000...

SELLER: They said if I wanted a quick sale, £145,000 for a quick sale.

JOHN: On the open market.

And the market's changed a bit. So what I'll do is speak to my investors, 'cause they are buying quite a few properties at the moment.

Because it's coming to Christmas, it's slowing down there, so what you want to do is get a committed sale before Christmas and then complete and in the next couple of months you'll be able to take that money.

Once the investor gives you about £101,000, after paying off your mortgage you're still left with £36,000. Obviously they would have to do the research first, If it's worth less than, let's just say for example, that the investors do their research and it's only worth £130,000, then the offer would be about £91,000. So it depends on what the valuation of the property is.

Appendix B - A Real Sale Word-By-Word

But still at £91,000 you'd be left with £26,000, so it's a bit of a nest egg. And I guess for you it's more the hassle as opposed to... (Here I was exerting my authority as a consultant who knows how this works)

SELLER: Yeah, yeah, I just want it done and gone and move on from this phase of my life.

JOHN: Well, you're not the first person to call us in this situation. We get people all the time who call us, they've bought the property thirty years ago and it's worth half a million but they're quite happy to accept less because they know that they can take that money and enjoy it.

Because that's what it's about, isn't it? It's about taking that money. (Selling the "pleasure" of having cash right now)

SELLER: Yeah, and the weight of worry off your shoulders means a lot. I haven't got the money, I can't do it, don't want it anymore.

JOHN: Okay, what I need to do is let me speak to an investor and make sure that they're happy to offer you the £101,000 or the discount based on what it's worth. So if it's worth £145,000, you'll get about £101,000. If it's worth £130,000, you'll get about £91,000. (Third person authority)

SELLER: Right, yeah.

JOHN: If our investor says yes, are you happy with that? (Test closing)

SELLER: Yep.

JOHN: What I need to do then is when would be a good time for one of our investors to pop round this week? Or next week?

Appendix B - A Real Sale Word-By-Word

SELLER: Is Sunday any good or is that too soon? (Shows the seller is very keen)

JOHN: No, Sunday will be good. It will probably be me who will be calling you back. So Franco will give you a call back and arrange for a time. I'll pass your number onto him and then he can arrange all that.

Also as part of this, they'll also pay for your legal fees and your survey, so we can put that into the paperwork for you. (Taking away the seller's "pain")

SELLER: Yeah, that'd be great, yeah.

JOHN: At least that'll save you a couple of grand then.

SELLER: Yeah.

JOHN: What Franco is going to do is, bring you some paperwork to say that if your property is worth either £145,000 or £130,000, your offer will be between £101,000 and £91,000.

And also we'll put in the paperwork as well that we'll cover all the legal fees and all the bits and pieces. Is that okay? (The legal fees is the "icing on the cake" and I deliberately saved it till last)

SELLER: Yeah, that sounds great. Thanks ever so much for your help.

The deal was closed and John, the seller, was happy. Dealing with motivated sellers such as the dialogue above is something we do day in day out at our office.

Property is a numbers game – the more people you speak to, the more deals you'll do.

Further Resources

If you wish to pursue your property education further, we run specialist training courses in the UK and can tailor specialist training to tailor your needs in any country.

Call us on +44 (0)1908 69 88 73 send an email to *Andy@ WealthDragons.co.uk.*

In the meantime, you may go to the following web sites for further resources and information:

www.WealthDragons.co.uk - Our main web site where you'll find all our products and services

www.WealthDragonsUnleashed.co.uk - For news about local networking events

www.LearnLeaseOptions.co.uk - For news and information about lease options

www.WealthDragons.co.uk/bootcamp.htm - To book places on our exclusive property boot camp courses

www.NetworkPropertyInvestment.co.uk - Find information on the forum and check out our latest below market value leads and packaged deals

www.WealthDragons.co.uk/npb.htm - Information about packaged leads